Have You Passed
the DNA Test?

Have You Passed the DNA Test?

Dr David E. Carr

New Wine Press

New Wine Ministries
PO Box 17
Chichester
West Sussex
United Kingdom
PO19 2AW

Copyright © 2010 Dr David E. Carr

All rights reserved. No part of this publication may be reproduced, stored in a retrieval system, or transmitted in any form or by any means, electronic, mechanical, photocopying or otherwise, without the prior written consent of the publisher. Short extracts may be used for review purposes.

Scripture quotations are taken from the following versions of the Bible:

NIV – Holy Bible, New International Version. Copyright © 1973, 1978, 1984 by International Bible Society. Used by permission of Hodder and Stoughton Limited.

NKJV – New King James Version. Copyright © 1982 by Thomas Nelson Inc. Used by permission. All rights reserved.

NASB – NEW AMERICAN STANDARD BIBLE®, Copyright©1960, 1962, 1963, 1968, 1971, 1972, 1973, 1975, 1977, 1995 by The Lockman Foundation. Used by permission.

KJV – King James Version. Copyright © 1967 by Oxford University Press Inc.

The Message – The Message. Copyright © 1993, 1994, 1995, 1996, 2000, 2001, 2002. Used by permission of NavPress Publishing Group.

The Amplified Bible – the Amplified® Bible, Copyright © 1954, 1958, 1962, 1964, 1965, 1987 by The Lockman Foundation. Used by permission.

CEV – Contemporary English Version Copyright © 1995 American Bible Society.

ESV – English Standard Version Copyright © 2001 Crossway Bibles.

ISBN 978-1-905991-54-9

Typeset by **documen**, www.documen.co.uk
Cover design by CCD, www.ccdgroup.co.uk
Printed in United Kingdom

Contents

	Introduction	7
Chapter 1	Amazing Grace	9
Chapter 2	Freedom of Faith	27
Chapter 3	Wonders of His Word	41
Chapter 4	Abundant Life	55
Chapter 5	Sanctification: The Power of the Spiritual Life	67
Chapter 6	The Fulfilment of Forgiveness	81
Chapter 7	Unspeakable Joy	95
Chapter 8	The Ultimate Expression of Giving and Receiving	111
Chapter 9	Mercy	123
Chapter 10	Tangible Peace	135
Chapter 11	Living Holiness	153
Chapter 12	Essential Truth	165
Chapter 13	Divine Compassion	183
Chapter 14	Righteousness	199
Chapter 15	Integrity	211
Chapter 16	Majestic Glory	225

THANKS

My thanks go to Anthea Towler and Alison Cannan for their proof reading and checking of scripture quotations.

INTRODUCTION

After spending years dealing with people and noticing how often the characteristics of their parents play a considerable part in their lifestyle, I have come to realise that it's not just the time spent with their parents that has fashioned them, it's all about DNA.

This code is a "blueprint" that we inherit from our parents. It can affect looks, mannerisms, hereditary complaints. Am I then a clone? No, there are enough of our individual traits to make us unique. Simply put, we cannot deny our formation, but our future lies firmly in our own hands.

This started me thinking about my Christian faith. If God is my Father, am I fashioned by His DNA? What characteristics of the divine are inbred in me? We are told in Matthew 7:20 that,

> *"Just as you can identify a tree by its fruit, so you can identify people by their actions."*   NLT

The "fruit of His Spirit" is basically the DNA of Christ Jesus. The degree to which people can see the manifestation of His nature in us, confirms or denies His Fatherhood of us.

I pray that this simple study of the characteristics of the Lord's DNA will stir within you a desire to be just like the Father.

Dr David Carr
January 2010

CHAPTER 1

Amazing Grace

*"The law tells me how crooked I am.
Grace comes along and straightens me out."*

—DL Moody

Many of us know about the amazing grace we are offered in and through relationship with Jesus, but we find it hard to accept it for ourselves. I honestly believe that if we could understand the grace of God it would transform our lives, change the places we live and alter the entire state of the nation! I just wonder what God's got to do to convince us that He tells the truth about His grace. We smile and say "Amen", but often we don't really believe it! We're not living, any of us, in the *fullness* of the grace of God.

If you think about it, we spend a lot of our time actually rejecting God's grace. Pastors do it, leaders do it, we all do it. Don't get me wrong here, I'm not getting at you, I'm just trying to help you understand God's heart towards you. Jesus laid His life down to pour His favour on us so that we could be His favourites – so that we could live life to the full. It must break His heart when we walk around lying to ourselves about who we are and the place we have in His heart.

This divine favour is not something we can earn or deserve, and good job too! Harry Ironside, an American pastor and preacher in the late 19th Century said, "Grace is the very opposite of merit ... Grace is not only undeserved favour, but it is favour shown to the one who has deserved the very opposite."

It's something only our perfect God can give. Grace means "benevolence to inferiors". Isn't that incredible? None of us is owed anything from God. *All* that He gives us is a free gift. God chooses to have fellowship with inferiors and His grace allows us to be on a level where we are accepted and acceptable to Him.

When the understanding of true grace is absent we can believe two extremes:

1) I'm nobody

Maybe this is sometimes how you feel. Perhaps you constantly compare yourself unfavourably with others and struggle not to believe your own "bad press". The script in your head always runs the same kind of tape: "I'm stupid, why can't I be like so-and-so? ... Can't I ever get things right? ... I'm a nobody ... why would God love me? ... I've done terrible things ..." I say this to you in love: STOP! You're not doing yourself any good! What's going on in your life, is that you have rejected God's grace for you and His heart for you. You're just not living in the abundance of Christ. But God's grace is there for you. Take it!

2) I'm really somebody amazing!

This is also a lie! It makes me angry when I see arrogant people puffing themselves up, believing they don't need God's favour or grace. The Bible is very clear about our place before God. Without Him, we are nothing. As the Israel Houghton song, *Friend of God,* begins: "Who am I, that you are mindful of me?"

Jeremiah 9:23-24 (NIV) says:

"This is what the LORD says: 'Let not the wise man boast of his wisdom or the strong man boast of his strength or the rich man boast of his riches, but let him who boasts boast about this: that he understands and knows me.'"

It's self-assessment day when we understand what God's grace is. We need to ask the question, "Who am I?" This isn't a "pity me" kind of "who am I?", it's an audit, and at times we all need to do that. Some of us are living in sin because we don't believe God has changed us *or* we believe He has already finished! Neither of these is true! Both of these are sinful positions, the first because it rejects the very power of God to transform and the second because it denies our need of Him.

But when we see who we are in the grace of Christ and what He's done for us, we can go before God as *somebody*. The grace of God is about living in His favour. It is God treating us as if we are winners, not losers. Maybe we need to start treating ourselves in the same way?

Living in God's favour

Born in 1725, John Newton was a slave trader. One night a violent storm swept huge waves over his ship. Moments after he left the deck, a crewman who'd taken his place was flung overboard and killed. Newton had to man the vessel for the remainder of the tempest. That one incident made him realise his helplessness. He concluded this: only the grace of God saved him that night. Only the favour of God had rescued him.

Newton read Thomas à Kempis' book *The Imitation of Christ*, and took his first step towards accepting faith in Jesus

Christ. Three years after his marriage, he suffered a stroke which prevented him ever going back to sea. Even though God worked on him, it took him forty years, in the culture in which he lived, to denounce slavery. He was ordained in June 1764 to the parish of Olney and, as a new curate, met the poet William Cowper who had just become a Christian himself. They became close friends, which led to the collaboration of them writing a poem called *Amazing Grace*, based on the scripture from 1 Chronicles 17:16-17:

> *"Then King David went in and sat before the LORD; and he said: 'Who am I, O LORD God? And what is my house, that You have brought me this far? And yet this was a small thing in Your sight, O God; and You have also spoken of Your servant's house for a great while to come, and have regarded me according to the rank of a man of high degree, O LORD God.'"*
>
> (NKJV)

What a wonderful set of truths is contained in this scripture! Newton, who transported slaves and saw himself as the lowest of the low, saw here the essence of God's undeserved favour. His understanding brought us those beautifully timeless and healing words:

> "Amazing grace, how sweet the sound
> that saved a wretch like me.
> I once was lost, but now I'm found,
> was blind but now I see."

Newton actually embraced this grace for himself. He didn't just write a song about it, this understanding of living in God's favour took him on a journey from drunken, cruel, slave-trader to humble, world-renowned preacher.

Grace is not a stand-alone attribute. If you read your Bible, you will see it linked to so many other characteristics of God. Grace and faith; grace and truth; grace and righteousness; grace and love; grace and peace; grace and mercy; grace and power.

If you are having problems in your life you need to look closely. Where is your truth? Where is your righteousness? Where is your love? Where is your peace? Where is your mercy? Where is your power? If you have plenty of those things the chances are that grace is reigning in your life.

In his book, *Transforming Grace,* (NavPress, 1991) Jerry Bridges says:

"God's grace does not negate the need for responsible action on our part, but rather makes it possible."

We all know the hymn I've just mentioned, *Amazing Grace*, but Newton's friend, William Cowper, also wrote a hymn and one verse says this:

> "Judge not the Lord by feeble sense,
> But trust Him for His grace;
> Behind a frowning providence
> He hides a smiling face."

You might think that God's angry with you, but behind that frown, which He must give towards sin, there's a smile of grace within. He can save you from what is eating away at your life. He can heal you from that soul sickness. Amazing grace! How sweet the sound, that saved a wretch like me!

Do you know God's favour on your life? Are you thankful? Do you know what it is to be benevolent to those who are beneath you because that's how He has treated you? This is the heart of amazing grace.

Let's look again at that last scripture from 1 Chronicles 17 and see what lessons in grace we can learn from the life of David:

a) awareness of self

David comes before the Lord aware that he is not worthy of His love, mercy or favour. "Who am I, O Lord?" he says. The day that we forget to say that, we've lost it! When we mistake ourselves for the main attraction, the main preacher or the main musician, we need to remember again who we are and where we have come from!

David makes here a positive confession of a majestic grace. He genuinely couldn't understand why God would do such wonderful things for him. He saw himself as a simple shepherd boy. Yet God favoured him; He called him and exalted him as king. What about his background? He wasn't living on the best side of town and he was the very last of his brothers to be presented before Samuel. He had no real influence. His brothers did not recommend him as a soldier to Saul when Goliath needed fighting, this was left to a servant! In his early life, he was largely forgotten, and yet his whole story speaks of a real understanding of who God is. He knew that God would bless whom He wanted to bless, and exalt whom He wanted to exalt. He knew that God could take dirt and make man out of it!

So He can take us and make anything out of us!

b) awareness of sin

David, having led a privileged life under the blessings, grace and favour of God, still committed adultery. He went up on a roof one day and saw a beautiful woman – Bathsheba – as she bathed. David began to lust after her, had her brought to him, got her pregnant and arranged for her husband to be killed.

It's surprising what people will do once sin has got into their lives in this way. We can find ourselves doing things we would never have contemplated six months before. But sin produces sin.

It was only after a prophet came to him and said, "God knows exactly what you're doing," that David was brought to the point of realising the state of his own heart. Charles H Spurgeon, a Baptist preacher, said this:

"Sometimes a sinner parleys with his Saviour, wishing he could have a little of the honour of his salvation, wanting to keep some favourite sin and amend the humbling terms of grace. But Jesus will be all in all, and the sinner must be nothing at all."

This is what David said to God:

"Against You, You only, have I sinned and done that which is evil in your sight."
(Psalm 51:4 Amplified Bible)

David knew that his actions had been wrong and that he had damaged his relationship with God. He humbled himself and made himself nothing before his creator.

c) awareness of separation
David also said,

"Do not cast me from Your presence."
(Psalm 51:11, NIV)

He knew well that sin separates us from God. How often do we try and argue our way out of this kind of thinking: "It's not my fault … It was the woman … the man … the church … my family …" But David is clear. He knew *he* was at fault and he knew God could choose to withdraw from him.

d) awareness of the Spirit
Then David said something else which is a little frightening:

> *"Do not take Your Holy Spirit from me."*
> (Psalm 51:11, NKJV)

I spent two years of my life with the Holy Spirit "taken from me" and I don't know how I can ever describe to you what a terrible life I had for that time. I didn't commit adultery or steal, but I disobeyed God and He chose to withdraw from me. For two years I had no consciousness of God in my life. I'm telling you now, and I say this in the reverence of God, for His sake don't *ever* go there. It's worse than being a non-Christian. A non-Christian has never known the presence of God, but when you've known Him and He withdraws, you're left in such a mess. I can tell you the day He went and I can tell you the day He came back. I can picture now the day He came back. I was sitting there in the big chair on the platform, the sun was coming through and it warmed my face, and God said in a semi-audible voice, "I am back. Don't you ever do that to me again."

e) awareness of salvation
David then asks for the restoration found in the saving grace of God:

> *"Restore to me the joy of your salvation."*
> (Psalm 51:12 NIV)

I have to ask myself the question, if there's not much joy in your life, are you truly saved? We all go through bad times which affect us: sickness and ill-health, divorce and death. But that isn't the question. Have you got joy in your life? David lost it and said, "Restore it back to me. Help me remember again what it feels like to know your salvation." Often, this is the key to joy being given back to us. Do you know this joy today?

Then David says, "What shall I do for God now? I shall teach men and instruct them and I will tell them about your goodness." He restored the relationship and wanted (like Newton) to put what he had learnt into practice. Verse 13 says:

> *"Then I will teach transgressors your ways, and sinners will turn back to you."*

Later in verse 17 he declares:

> *"The sacrifices of God are a broken spirit; a broken and contrite heart, O God, you will not despise."*

Jonathan Edwards, the American revivalist, said:

> *"Grace is but glory begun, and glory is but grace perfected."*

Grace in the New Testament

There are 154 occurrences in the New Testament of the word *charis* or grace – and most are found in the Pauline letters. Paul often majors on the undeserved favour of God.

Here, Paul gives a benediction, a long expression of God's mercy and goodness.

> *"Blessed be the God and Father of our Lord Jesus Christ, who has blessed us with every spiritual blessing in the heavenly places in Christ, just as He chose us in Him before the foundation of the world, that we should*

be holy and without blame before Him in love, having predestined us to adoption as sons by Jesus Christ to Himself, according to the good pleasure of His will, to the praise of the glory of His grace, by which He made us accepted in the Beloved.

In Him we have redemption through His blood, the forgiveness of sins, according to the riches of His grace which He made to abound toward us in all wisdom and prudence, having made known to us the mystery of His will, according to His good pleasure which He purposed in Himself, that in the dispensation of the fullness of the times He might gather together in one all things in Christ, both which are in heaven and which are on earth—in Him. In Him also we have obtained an inheritance, being predestined according to the purpose of Him who works all things according to the counsel of His will, that we who first trusted in Christ should be to the praise of His glory.

In Him you also trusted, after you heard the word of truth, the gospel of your salvation; in whom also, having believed, you were sealed with the Holy Spirit of promise, who is the guarantee of our inheritance until the redemption of the purchased possession, to the praise of His glory."

(Ephesians 1:3-14 NKJV)

Paul, who described himself as the "chief of sinners", knew first-hand the beauty of grace in his own life.

"In him we have redemption through his blood, the forgiveness of sins, in accordance with the riches of God's grace that he lavished on us with all wisdom and understanding."

(Ephesians 1:7-8 NIV)

"In Him..." is the key that Paul understood. In ourselves we have no righteousness; we're like filthy rags. But "in Him" we are redeemed and bought back. The Christian experience is referred to through many metaphors: born again, adopted, redeemed, chosen ... This is the act of a Creator who once made us in His own image then shed His own blood, the blood of Jesus Christ, to make us into His new creation, restoring the relationship with the Father at a cost beyond money.

The riches of this grace are limitless. We are not only redeemed from the slavery of sin by His blood, but forgiven daily by the wealth and abundance of His grace and favour. Jesus showed this amazing grace to the extortionist Zacchaeus (Luke 19), to the condemned thief on the cross (Luke 23:42), to the woman caught in adultery (John 8:3), and to countless others.

And now He shows it to you.

We've been bought back, made whole and given what we could never have dreamt of or deserved.

Does grace allow us to keep sinning?

Some of us have such a wrong concept of grace. We think it will give us licence to do just as we please. But Paul is very clear about this:

> *"Well then, should we keep on sinning so that God can show us more and more of his wonderful grace? Of course not! Since we have died to sin, how can we continue to live in it?....*
> *Well then, since God's grace has set us free from the law, does that mean we can go on sinning? Of course not! Don't you realize that you become the slave of whatever you choose to obey? You can be a slave to*

sin, which leads to death, or you can choose to obey God, which leads to righteous living. Thank God! Once you were slaves of sin, but now you wholeheartedly obey this teaching we have given you. Now you are free from your slavery to sin, and you have become slaves to righteous living.

Because of the weakness of your human nature, I am using the illustration of slavery to help you understand all this. Previously, you let yourselves be slaves to impurity and lawlessness, which led ever deeper into sin. Now you must give yourselves to be slaves to righteous living so that you will become holy.

When you were slaves to sin, you were free from the obligation to do right. And what was the result? You are now ashamed of the things you used to do, things that end in eternal doom. But now you are free from the power of sin and have become slaves of God. Now you do those things that lead to holiness and result in eternal life. For the wages of sin is death, but the free gift of God is eternal life through Christ Jesus our Lord."

(Extracts from Romans 6:1-23 NLT)

There's a deep error in many Christians' thinking today about grace. Some of us have the concept as "Born again Evangelicals" that grace allows us to do things that we'd have been punished for in the Old Testament. Let me briefly address this misconception.

The Old Testament was very clear about the punishments for violating God's law. Some people believe that, under the grace and divine favour we find in the New Testament, our God is consistently tolerant, forgiving and accepting; that He doesn't really MIND about our sin any more. This is totally untrue! If you believe that, you've got to get yourself sorted out!

We hear excuses for poor behaviour in the Church all the time. "They were sidetracked ... they took their eye off the ball ... they were attacked by the devil ... they gave way under deep pressure ..." etc. Such violations are no longer seen as "sin" and of course, we also hear people in the same breath saying, "We must show them grace and we mustn't judge."

John Piper, a pastor in Minnesota, said this:

"Grace is not simply leniency when we have sinned. Grace is the enabling gift of God *not to sin*. Grace is power, not just pardon."

Expensive grace

God's grace is no cheap option. It has to be sought with tears. We are saved by grace through faith.

> *"For by grace you have been saved through faith, and that not of yourselves; it is the gift of God, not of works, lest anyone should boast."*
> (Ephesians 2:8-9 NKJV)

Paul tells us that through faith in Christ Jesus we have been released from the penalty of death, therefore we have no mandate to sin any more. Grace brings the ability to live a life fulfilling the law *and* living in the favour of God. Look at this passage from Romans:

> *"...knowing that Christ, having been raised from the dead, dies no more. Death no longer has dominion over Him. For the death that He died, He died to sin once for all; but the life that He lives, He lives to God. Likewise you also, reckon yourselves to be dead indeed to sin, but alive to God in Christ Jesus our Lord.*

Therefore do not let sin reign in your mortal body, that you should obey it in its lusts. And do not present your members as instruments of unrighteousness to sin, but present yourselves to God as being alive from the dead, and your members as instruments of righteousness to God. For sin shall not have dominion over you, for you are not under law but under grace.
What then? Shall we sin because we are not under law but under grace? Certainly not! Do you not know that to whom you present yourselves slaves to obey, you are that one's slaves whom you obey, whether of sin leading to death, or of obedience leading to righteousness? But God be thanked that though you were slaves of sin, yet you obeyed from the heart that form of doctrine to which you were delivered. And having been set free from sin, you became slaves of righteousness."

(Romans 6:9-18 NKJV)

Grace demands a higher level of living

So don't you dare say to me, "We're under grace now … we can do what we like!"

The Law gave no personal relationship with the Messiah, but grace did. The Law had no redemptive power, but grace had. The Law could not bring forgiveness, but grace could. The Law gave no access to the Holy of Holies, but grace takes us beyond the veil and sits us in the mercy seat. The Law could only remind us of our failure, but grace reminds us of the Lord's success. Grace is the ability to deliver a life of greater integrity and passion; the expectation of success is higher – I can do all things through Christ who strengthens me!

"You have heard that it was said to those of old, '*You shall not commit adultery*'" – describes the Law.

> *"But I say to you that whoever looks at a woman to lust for her has already committed adultery with her in his heart"* – describes Grace.
> (Matthew 5:27-28 NKJV)

The law says, "Do not commit adultery." Grace says, "Do not lust." Not many of us have committed "actual" adultery but everybody has lusted after another person to some degree. God expects us to live at a higher level under grace than we did under law.

> *"You have heard that it was said to those of old, 'You shall not murder, and whoever murders will be in danger of the judgment.' But I say to you that whoever is angry with his brother without a cause shall be in danger of the judgment."*
> (Matthew 5:21-22 NKJV)

Why does God set the level higher under grace? I believe the reason is that under the Law His people never knew His name – we do. Under the Law they didn't know the power of the cross – we do. Under the Law He wasn't living *in* them – but He lives in us. With all that, grace means we can now live a victorious life. We don't have to submit our mortal bodies to sin and we do not have to let sin have dominion over us. We can be victorious in Christ!

This does not mean we become sinless. John Wesley had a good way of explaining it. He didn't believe in sinless perfection, but he did believe we would sin less. If you're still committing the same sins and have the same bad attitudes as you had ten years ago, where's the evidence of grace in your life? Grace is the ability to rise above those sins. Perhaps you need to get some prayer?

The character of Jesus

The Bible makes it clear that Jesus, the Word, was Himself full of grace. Every action and every word personified what grace was and is:

> *"The Word became flesh and made his dwelling among us. We have seen his glory, the glory of the One and Only, who came from the Father, full of grace and truth."*
>
> *"John testifies concerning him. He cries out, saying, 'This was he of whom I said, "He who comes after me has surpassed me because he was before me." From the fullness of his grace we have all received one blessing after another. For the law was given through Moses; grace and truth came through Jesus Christ."*
>
> (John 1:14-17 NIV)

And after the Law came through Moses, grace came through Jesus. Moses says, "You've got it wrong!" and Jesus says, "I can put it right!" Law says that you're going to die; Christ says, "I can keep you alive!"

> *"Moreover the law entered that the offence might abound. But where sin abounded, grace abounded much more, so that as sin reigned in death, even so grace might reign through righteousness to eternal life through Jesus Christ our Lord."*
>
> (Romans 5:20-21 NKJV)

By grace, through faith, God will do for you what you don't deserve and give to you that which nobody else can. He'll change you in a way that nobody else can change you. He'll love you with a love that nobody else can love you with. That's why it's amazing grace!

May you know this abundant and amazing grace flowing through your life today. Amen.

Thinking it through:

Dale Ralph Davies said, "It is not only by grace alone that we become God's people, but by grace alone we remain His people." (*1 Samuel*, Christian Focus Publications, 1988, p. 129.)

◊ What signs are there in your life that God's grace is at work?
◊ Do you know the sense of God's favour and blessing over you right now?
◊ What is the evidence for this?
◊ What do you think you need to work on, in your mind and heart, in order to allow God's grace more access in your life?

CHAPTER 2
Freedom of Faith

There are only two references to the word "faith" in the Old Testament (Deuteronomy 32:20 and Habakkuk 2:4). Why is it that the Old Testament is not full of verses connected to this important biblical principle? The answer is because faith comes by *hearing* and hearing by *the Word of God as revealed in Jesus* (see Romans 10:17). People often think that faith is a "gift" for the few, but in fact it's given to every Christian.

The dictionary defines faith as "secure belief in God and a trusting acceptance of His will". Faith, then, is having confidence in and a true reliance on God. I wonder what your faith levels are like today? What are the things that exercise your heart and cause you to doubt? I pray that God uses the words of this chapter to encourage and bless you, to strengthen and empower you to rise up with more faith than you have ever had before! The kind of faith I'm talking about is not dull or inactive – it is explosive and cannot be subdued; it rises up, making itself both visible and productive. Faith is the realisation of things hoped for, the evidence of things not seen.

Thomas Aquinas, who died in 1274, described the sort of faith I mean:

"To one who has faith, no explanation is necessary. To one without faith, no explanation is possible."

In other words, if you have faith, nobody needs to explain anything of God to you. You hear or see something godly and your spirit just says, "Amen! I agree." I *know*, for instance, that God heals sick people. Don't try and ask me to explain why or how. I don't know! I just know by faith that He does. I've seen the blind see, the lame walk and cancers inexplicably leave people's bodies. I've even seen God give people new hearts! You can't explain that to me and I can't explain it to you. If you are reading this with no access to God's faith then whatever I say, you won't believe! You'll read this with scepticism or put it down altogether. If you don't have faith then no explanation or evidence I offer will give you faith. But if you've got faith then you won't need any confirmation at all.

I believe we should be seeing more miracles in our lives and in our churches. I get so excited about it! If we honestly believe that the fullness of God dwells in Jesus Christ, then we can do all things through Him. John 14:9 says:

"Anyone who has seen me has seen the Father." NIV

If we have faith in Jesus, as our Saviour, friend and elder brother, then we have access to all the resources of heaven. So what is it that stops us from seeing amazing miracles and being amazing people? I think it's often simply down to our lack of faith.

It's interesting that some people seem to have more faith than others. But faith is not something that we can generate or work up within ourselves. We are not Christians because of any kind of self-generated belief. Faith is a spiritual implantation of God.

Faith comes by hearing

All of us live by natural belief in certain things, but this is not the same as faith. Natural belief comes through the assurance of a number of circumstances that have proven positive. What do I mean? You have faith to fly because the law of averages says very few airplanes crash. You go to hospital and you meet a doctor you've never met before. You don't know anything about him and you sign a piece of paper, submitting yourself to an operation you don't fully understand. You hope you'll come out the other side and live again. This is belief, but it's certainly not God's faith. God's faith is not based on our natural sense of what is likely to happen:

> *"So then faith comes by hearing, and hearing by the word of God."*
>
> (Romans 10:17 NKJV)

Isn't it interesting that what you hear either demoralises you or blesses you? What you hear either builds you up or pulls you down. What you hear has an effect on you. When you hear somebody talking about you it upsets you or it delights you. Hearing plays a huge part in our attitudes. We either become de-motivated or excited. The Bible says that divine belief comes by *hearing about* Jesus. Galatians 3:2 (ESV) says,

> *"Let me ask you only this: Did you receive the Spirit by works of the law or by **hearing with faith**?"*

Verse 5 says,

> *"Does he who supplies the Spirit to you and works miracles among you do so by works of the law, or by hearing with faith?"*

Incredible things come by *hearing with faith*. Some people visit our church and nothing changes in their lives. They look at their watches and wait to go home again. But the person next to them may receive an incredible miracle of healing or blessing. God is available to both kinds of people, but only one kind is really "hearing with faith".

Faith to believe

Faith is manifested in different forms. First, there's a faith to believe. You cannot become a Christian by just praying a prayer, coming out to the front or putting your hand up. That in itself doesn't make you a Christian. Faith is when you get to a point in your life where you say, "I want to believe in You and I want to receive You and I want this dynamic belief factor in my life." You do this when the Holy Spirit comes to you and convicts you of sin, righteousness and the judgement to come. You say, "Yes please. I don't know exactly what's happening, but I know it's God and I am responding."

A man came to see me the other day. I asked, "How did you become a Christian?" He said, "Funnily enough, two years ago on a Tuesday night, my sister brought me here. She doesn't come to this church, but she said, "My church won't help you but I know a church that will."

He went on, "I've got a criminal record and I've mucked my life up and I tried three times to come through that door and I couldn't. I forced myself in and sat right at the back. Before you prayed for the sick you preached and said that people needed to give their lives to Christ. You said, 'Come forward' then you said, 'Sorry, there's a man over in this area, you've tried to come into this building three times tonight and you've not been able to.' I knew that was me and suddenly my heart started racing. Then you said, 'David, get out of your seat and run forward!' That's my name and so I ran forward. That night I got born again!"

As soon as David heard that word for him, he experienced a sense of being filled with the faith to believe. He did not become a Christian by joining a church, being baptised or just coming out at an altar call. He was spoken to, dramatically and personally, by the Holy Spirit. He chose to respond. Faith to believe does not always happen in the same way. People will experience many different sensations (or no sensations at all) when they find the faith to believe for the first time.

We cannot simply believe on our own because the Bible says,

> *"For by grace you have been saved through faith, and that not of yourselves; it is the gift of God, not of works, lest anyone should boast."*
> (Ephesians 2:8-9 NKJV)

As we respond to the conviction of the Holy Spirit, faith is implanted in the heart of humankind and then,

> *"Whoever calls on the name of the LORD shall be saved."* (Romans 10:13 NKJV)

This faith to believe is a gift from Almighty God; it does not come from what *we* do.

I heard somebody completely ridicule a female politician recently because she said she believed in creation. There is no way you can believe in creation other than by faith. But when you become a Christian, by faith, you can immediately believe in creation, the resurrection, the virgin birth and in the authority of Scripture, because you know the Author and you trust His word.

So rather than getting annoyed and uptight when the evolutionists argue their case, or the sceptics throw doubt on yet another Bible story, we need to remember that faith is a gift and without it people are simply blind to the truth.

Faith to receive

There is a faith that reveals and allows us to receive the very nature of Christ.

> *"But the fruit of the Spirit is love, joy, peace, longsuffering, kindness, goodness, faithfulness, gentleness, self-control."*
> (Galatians 5:22-23 NKJV)

These attributes are the defined nature of Jesus. Jesus' "DNA" is transferred to believers at their conversion. That's why they were first called "Christians" at Antioch, because they were seen to be "like Christ". When you become a committed Christian, God's nature becomes part of you:

> *"For to one is given the word of wisdom through the Spirit, to another the word of knowledge through the same Spirit, to another faith by the same Spirit."*
> (1 Corinthians 12:8-9 NKJV)

Faith to succeed

Not only do we have faith to believe and faith to receive His nature, but we are also given the faith to *achieve*. This is the kind of faith that causes us to lay hands on the sick, or takes us out of well-paid employment to work with street children.

This is the faith that causes churches to be planted and lives to be changed. This faith allows us to keep going even if we get disillusioned. It is the faith that Christ endured the cross with.

This faith defends us from the spiritual aggression of a fallen world. It's the:

> *"shield of faith."* (Ephesians 6:16 NKJV)

Sometimes, when everything's going against you, you need to put up that shield and say, "Listen, I don't care what goes wrong ... God is with me."

Faith in the New Testament

There are 243 references to faith in the New Testament, over half of them made by Paul:

> *"For I am not ashamed of the gospel of Christ, for it is the power of God to salvation for everyone who believes, for the Jew first and also for the Greek."*
> (Romans 1:16 NKJV)

> *"For since, in the wisdom of God, the world through wisdom did not know God, it pleased God through the foolishness of the message preached to save those who believe. For Jews request a sign, and Greeks seek after wisdom; but we preach Christ crucified, to the Jews a stumbling block and to the Greeks foolishness, but to those who are called, both Jews and Greeks, Christ the power of God and the wisdom of God. Because the foolishness of God is wiser than men, and the weakness of God is stronger than men."*
> (1 Corinthians 1:21-25 NKJV)

Paul realised that the majority of people who surrounded him were not looking for true faith. He understood that the Greeks wanted worldly wisdom and the Jews were waiting for miraculous signs. A lot of people try out church with similar attitudes. Some want an answer to a problem and others want a miracle, but they might not get either unless they are given the gift of faith!

Hebrews 11 is the most amazing chapter about faith in the Bible. It lists the "heroes" of faith and tells us what they achieved, stressing over and over that it was BY FAITH. For example, it was by faith that Abel understood the sort of sacrifice God required. Faith like this enables us to know how to please God. It was by faith that Noah was divinely warned of the flood. Sometimes God will warn us that something challenging is on its way. How? By faith. It was by faith that Abraham obeyed when he was called leave his home. Why do we sometimes feel called to go out and start new things for God? It is by faith. It was by faith that Sarah became pregnant. There was no way she was going to become a shareholder in Mothercare! At her age she was a granny figure; she was not expected to be in a bed in the maternity wing! But by faith her whole life and outlook changed. The local headline could have read, "Shamed local pensioner becomes proud first-time mum!"

Faith for visions

But godly faith does not even have to produce visible, tangible evidence. Many great men and women of faith have died never seeing the fulfilment of their dream or vision. True faith gives us the freedom to look into the future at the promises of God and strive towards them, without needing their fulfilment to validate our belief system.

I've seen lots of visions come to pass, but I also have many dreams that haven't been fulfilled yet. God has told me that I won't ever see some of the things I have worked towards. I'll die before they happen. But I know that I don't have to see those things completed. I've seen the plans for an amazing cathedral which will one day be built on the site of our existing church, but I may never see it built. If it goes up 10 years after I've died, however, I won't be upset! I know what it looks like. When I'm in heaven I'm not going to be sitting there wishing I was in the cathedral, am I?

For 38 years I've had a vision of a church of 7,000 people in the heart of England. Have I actually seen it yet? No. We haven't got 7,000 people yet, but I had that vision when I was 27. I'm now 65. I still believe it will happen. But it may well not be in my lifetime.

The trouble is that we only tend to understand things in the "here and now". If we can't see things happening we think we must have got it wrong, or that God has got it wrong! But God says no, just keep walking in the vision. Faith means I haven't got to see it now. It's not mine, it's His. I'm only the manager. If He moves me to Head Office before the bonus is paid then that's fine with me! Somewhere, between now and then, I'll wake up one morning and think, "That's a bit of a bright light and realise where I am!"

Years ago I broke my nose and consequently I can't smell much. That's why I put so much aftershave on that it makes people cry! But when I get to heaven I'll smell the fragrance of paradise, I'll smell the flowers. I'll see God as He really is. And the Lord will say to me, "Do you want to see your vision fulfilled?" I honestly think I'll say, "No, I don't mind really. I'm just enjoying being with you!"

We shouldn't be disappointed with our life if all we get to do is live in faith. Faith is not the achievement of the few, it's the prerequisite of all believers and the passport to an amazing life. Faith took Abraham through the test of Isaac. Faith enabled Joseph to believe that one day his bones would be buried in the Promised Land. Faith changed Moses' mindset. Faith brought Jericho down. Faith saved Rahab.

> *"Without faith it is impossible to please Him, for he who comes to God must believe that He is, and that He is a rewarder of those who diligently seek Him."*
>
> (Hebrews 11:6 NKJV)

Faith is essentially an act of trust or reliance on God's convincing proof without demonstration. Jesus explained this kind of faith to Thomas:

> *"Blessed are those who have not seen and yet have believed."*
>
> (John 20:29 NKJV)

Speaking of the revelation of Christ, Peter says,

> *"Though now you do not see Him, yet believing, you rejoice with joy inexpressible and full of glory."*
>
> (1 Peter 1:8 NKJV)

Faith to be healed

Sometimes our faith will bring people to Jesus and offer them the chance to receive faith for themselves.

> *"Then behold, they brought to Him a paralytic lying on a bed. When Jesus saw their faith, He said to the paralytic, 'Son, be of good cheer; your sins are forgiven you.'"*
>
> (Matthew 9:2 NKJV)

Jesus saw the faith of the man's friends. This was the trigger for Him to act. Often people come to the church I'm involved in, bringing a friend in dire need of faith and help. Or perhaps they are desperate for healing, but can't get there themselves. I have seen many people given faith for their friends to be healed and God has honoured that.

Matthew chapter 9 contains another two healings where Jesus speaks of the faith of the person involved. Verse 22 describes a woman who had belief in the Word. Jesus would have worn a Rabbi's gown with a blue band around the hem signifying that He was a teacher of the Word. The woman chose to touch this:

> "Jesus turned and saw her. "Take heart, daughter," he said, "your faith has healed you." And the woman was healed from that moment." NIV

Then we read of two blind men who followed Jesus shouting,

> "Son of David, have mercy on me."

Verse 29-30 says:

> "Then he touched their eyes and said, 'According to your faith will it be done to you'; and their sight was restored."

So, by just looking at this one chapter, we can already see faith in action and the results it brings for those affected by severe illness.

The book of Acts also shows real manifestations of such faith. Peter explains the healing of a lame man saying that faith derives its strength through Jesus' name:

"Faith in Jesus' name put this man, whose condition you know so well, on his feet—yes, faith and nothing but faith put this man healed and whole right before your eyes." (Acts 3:16 The Message)

Faith to change

Mother Teresa of Calcutta said this:

"I know God will not give me anything I can't handle. I just wish that He didn't trust me so much."

What a beautiful statement! God not only trusts us, He will also never allow us to be overwhelmed. But we have to exercise our faith. Faith has to be active. Maybe you are reading this and realise what you most need is faith to change.

Perhaps you have got yourself into a difficult relationship and can't seem to get out. Maybe you are in the throws of a serious illness or are plagued by an addiction. What you need from God is the faith to change.

I challenged a woman recently who'd just been healed of cancer. She stood at the front of the church, beautiful and in her early thirties. I told her she needed to give her life to Christ and allow him to change her. She smiled and said, "I'm going on a holiday and when I come back, I'll do it." She went away, sat by the edge of the pool and died of a massive cerebral haemorrhage.

God wants to give you faith to believe in Him to such an extent that He can break the power of sin and sickness off your life. He can do it! We will never be truly free until God puts faith in us to believe.

Your heart is pumping every minute of the day; your brain is thinking every moment of the day; your kidneys are flushing every moment of the day. Your body is totally coordinated and your brain is sending messages all over, telling your body to fight disease and to resist illness. When you sleep your involuntary muscles keep working to keep your digestive system going. Your dream life, your subconscious, starts playing back the important things of the day for you and you start watching a replay and seeing weird pictures in the bank of your library.

You are so finely made! I don't mean to scare you, but at any moment any of these things could stop functioning. Every morning you wake up, is a new start and a fresh chance to have faith in God. Don't waste your life wondering what it would be like to know God better. Start today!

Thinking it through:

Patrick Overton said this:
"When you have come to the edge of all light that you know,
And are about to drop off into the darkness of the unknown,
Faith is knowing one of two things will happen:
There will be something solid to stand on or you will be taught to fly."

◊ What is your faith like today?
◊ Do you feel you need faith to believe for something specific?
◊ How do you feel your faith has changed in the last few months? Has it grown or diminished? Why do you think that is?
◊ What are some of the challenges that your faith has gone through recently? What has been the result?

Maybe you could use this prayer as you reflect on some of these questions:

"Father God, Your word injects faith into my heart. Faith comes by hearing and hearing by the Word. I'm asking You Lord, in Your kindness, in Your mercy, to forgive me for all in my life that does not reflect faith, and I'm asking you Lord, by Your grace and mercy, pour Your faith into my life: enough to move mountains, to deal with the issues in my life. Take away my fears, take away my phobias, take away my love of sinning. Become my faith, my belief and my faithfulness.

Amen."

CHAPTER 3
Wonders of His Word

What do we mean by God's Word?

God's word, as revealed in Scripture, is the most compelling and authoritative voice we can ever tune into. There are over 730 references to "the word" in the Bible. It is clearly something God sees as a priority for us to grasp and understand.

Deuteronomy 30:14 (NIV) declares:

> "...the word is very near you; it is in your mouth and in your heart so you may obey it."

Whenever God chooses to reveal something to us, it is always worth hearing and obeying. Throughout the Bible we see that when God speaks, amazing things happen. When God makes a promise that He will accomplish something, He never goes back on His word. His word *never* fails. What a wonderful guarantee that is!

God's word has power in and of itself. Revealing the very nature and heart of God, His voice fulfils His purposes and declares His truths. When God speaks, things are brought into being. His voice alone has the power to create something out of nothing.

When we read the Creation story in Genesis, we see that God produced the heavens and the earth simply by opening His mouth and declaring things into being. Ten times in the first chapter we read the words, "God said".

> *"And God said, 'Let there be light,' and there was light."* (Genesis 1:3 NIV)

It sounds so simple doesn't it? He spoke and there it was! If we really understood the power of His word, I honestly believe we would be different people. If we really took God *at* His word, imagine how our churches and communities would look!

The book of Hebrews teaches us that this power of God to create and sustain all life was achieved through the person of Jesus:

> *"He has spoken to us by his Son, whom he appointed heir of all things, and through whom he made the universe. The Son is the radiance of God's glory and the exact representation of his being, sustaining all things by his powerful word."* (Hebrews 1:2-3 NIV)

Sometimes we get excited about God but we don't completely understand what He is up to because we don't fully know and appreciate who He is. We can only know what has been revealed to us or what we have discovered. Did you realise today that your life is sustained by Jesus and His powerful word? Isn't that a fabulous thing to know?

The Bible makes it clear that not only is Jesus a channel of God's word and the "exact representation of His being" as we have just read, but also that He himself became THE WORD.

What does this mean for us today?

The word becomes flesh

I am getting to the age now where I can't remember everything people say to me. Sometimes I'll be preaching somewhere and a person will send their regards to someone I know. But I forget who, so I pass on half a message. The conversation will go a bit like this:

"I saw a guy last week who said to say hello to you."
"Is that right? Who was it?"
"I've no idea!"
I end up frustrating everyone!

It's really important to grasp the whole message of God and to remember the truths of His word. God's word *became a person* in the character and life of Jesus. He is described in a number of scriptures as THE word or *Logos*. John 1 explains who Jesus is and what His role is:

> *"In the beginning was the Word, and the Word was with God, and the Word was God. He was in the beginning with God. All things came into being through Him, and apart from Him nothing came into being that has come into being."*
>
> (John 1:1-3 NASB)

It is in and through Jesus that God accomplished not only creation – nothing was made without Him – but also our salvation. John 1:14 (NCV) then goes on to explain:

> *"The Word became a human and lived among us. We saw his glory—the glory that belongs to the only Son of the Father—and he was full of grace and truth."*

Whenever we look at Jesus or hear His words, we are looking at and hearing the word of God made human. It is the power of these words that creates faith in us to turn to and hope in the resurrection of Jesus.

As Romans 10:17 (NIV) says:

"Consequently, faith comes from hearing the message, and the message is heard through the word of Christ."

Name recognition

Some cultures have far more of a defining dependency on their choice of names than we do. Our culture picks names for our children for many reasons. But very rarely in Western society do we in choose a name because of its meaning.

But names are important, aren't they? When your name is mentioned it will conjure up many things to many people. What do people know you for? Are you the life and soul of the party? ... the negative one? ... the generous person? ... someone known for your wisdom or gentleness? What does the mention of your name bring to people's minds?

When you know someone's name, you can call it and they can choose to answer or to ignore you! Isn't it frustrating when you forget someone's name? You rack your brain for hours and it doesn't come back to you! But the Bible helps us out with this as far as God goes. Scripture is full of the names of God, helping us to both remember and understand more of His nature and His purpose. Who God is, is bound up in what He says and vice-versa.

Moses came to God with a very limited knowledge of who He was and what He was talking about. He literally did not have a clue! We can look at some of the questions he asked and think, with our slant on reading Scripture, that they are rhetorical. But I believe many of them are genuine, "Who are you anyway?", type questions.

In Exodus 3:13 Moses says to God:

> *"Suppose I go to the Israelites and say to them, 'The God of your fathers has sent me to you,' and they ask me, 'What is his name?' Then what shall I tell them?" God said to Moses, "I AM WHO I AM. This is what you are to say to the Israelites: 'I AM has sent me to you.'"* NIV

God shares here with Moses one of the most incredible of His names in the whole of Scripture. "I AM" is a name that has no boundaries, no limits and no definitions. It sums up the present, past and future of the word of God. Moses now knows all he needs to know to fulfil God's request of him to go to Pharaoh and ask for the release of the Israelites. He knows enough of God in that one name to realise that He is a force to be reckoned with and a powerful deliverer.

Sometimes I read about encounters like this with God and get really frustrated with myself. I mean, why aren't I ten times more able to perform great things for God than Moses was? I know all the names of the Lord. I even know the meaning of them! I know the power of them. I know that every one of His names is a stand-alone powerful key that can transform lives. I know Christ and the transforming work of the Holy Spirit in my life. I have the word of God in my heart and in my home in a way Moses never did, especially at the beginning of his journey. So why is it that I am not living a dynamic life like Moses where I regularly hear the audible voice of the living God? How much more of God have you and I got to understand before we can perform or receive such miracles? It makes you think doesn't it?

Moses didn't know much or any of those things. But still he managed to lead a million people out of slavery, communicate with a burning bush, part the Red Sea, strike a rock and release pure water, and send plagues on a nation. He did all this with only a limited knowledge of the word of God and the names God uses of Himself. Doesn't that astound you?

What does the Bible say about itself?

The best source of information about God's word is found in the Bible itself. It is very useful to study what it says about itself. Here are some of the characteristics of God's word as defined by Scripture:

1. The Word of God is always productive
The prophet Isaiah teaches us that the word of God never returns to Him empty, but has the habit of production.

> "The rain and snow come down from the heavens and stay on the ground to water the earth. They cause the grain to grow, producing seed for the farmer and bread for the hungry. It is the same with my word. I send it out, and it always produces fruit. It will accomplish all I want it to, and it will prosper everywhere I send it."
>
> (Isaiah 55:10-11 NLT)

God's word always has a destiny and a purpose and it will always fulfil what God desires it to.

2. The Word of God will never pass away
Isaiah 40: 8 (NASB) tells us:

> "The grass withers, the flower fades,
> But the word of our God stands forever."

Whatever happens to us or to the world we live in, God's word is of eternal strength, power and significance.

3. The Word of God can penetrate the heart of man
Hebrews 4:12 (NIV) reads:

> *"For the word of God is living and active. Sharper than any double-edged sword, it penetrates even to dividing soul and spirit, joints and marrow; it judges the thoughts and attitudes of the heart."*

The word of God can have an incredible impact on people. It can compel us, convict us, encourage, teach, inspire and guide us. As 2 Timothy 3:16 says:

> *"All Scripture is God-breathed and is useful for teaching, rebuking, correcting and training in righteousness."*

4. The Word of God brings light and revelation which sets people free
John 8:31-32 (NASB) explains,

> *"So Jesus was saying to those Jews who had believed Him, 'If you continue in My word, then you are truly disciples of Mine; and you will know the truth, and the truth will make you free.'"*

If we aim to stay tuned into God's word as His followers, we will understand the truths of His word and this will bring us great liberty.

5. The word of God makes us wise
Psalm 119:98-101 (NIV) tells us:

> *"Your commands make me wiser than my enemies, for they are ever with me. I have more insight than all my teachers, for I meditate on your statutes. I have more understanding than the elders, for I obey your precepts. I have kept my feet from every evil path so that I might obey your word."*

Sometimes we might be tempted to go to other people or other sources for our wisdom. But God's word is the anchor and the fountain of all knowledge and understanding.

6. The word of God brings us satisfying peace and stops us from falling
Psalm 119:165 (NIV) declares,

> *"Great peace have they who love your law, and nothing can make them stumble."*

We are able to live in trust and quietness of spirit when we know and understand what God is asking us to do.

How can we hear the word?

It is important that we learn how to handle the word of God well. We need to read it faithfully, weighing it up and studying it carefully. There is power, salvation, healing and deliverance in the word of God. All we need to know for life is contained in the pages of Scripture.

If we struggle to understand its meaning we need to seek advice and help. But as an anonymous author states, we must go to God first:

"There is a way of reading the Bible that seems to leave God far away, off in the shadows somewhere. It is all information and technicalities and knowledge, but it feels like you're sitting with your back towards God. You come up against a difficulty or question, and you go to books, you ask pastors, friends, strangers on the internet, anyone but Him. Gradually God gets smaller and dimmer." (Author unknown)

There is no doubt that we can find information from study guides, commentaries or those wiser than us in faith, but we need to remember that God's word is living and active. It is breathing and moving, not static and dead. If we are able to handle

"the sword of the Spirit, which is the word of God,"
(Ephesians 6:17 NKJV)

we will not be undermined when the enemy seeks to attack.

Satan's primary tactic is to cause us to doubt the word. Disbelief in the word of God is one of the most dangerously life-threatening things for any Christian. Often all the devil needs to do, as the serpent did with Eve in the garden of Eden, is to ask, "Did God really say that? Is His word true? Can you really trust that you heard Him?" to send us off course into mild panic.

Accessing God's word

We can hear the word of God in many different ways, not just through reading the Bible and taking time to listen to Him.

1. Through creation
The whole earth was brought into being by God's powerful word. All of creation speaks of God's glory and can speak to us (see Psalm 19:1-6).

2. Through others

God uses fellow believers to teach and encourage us. He may give them specific words of hope, encouragement or warning for us too.

3. Through preaching

As a preacher myself, I am always aware of how much God can speak to people through the words He gives me to bring to the church. Over the years, I have watched God accomplish many things in people's lives through the power of the spoken and preached word.

4. Through worship

God can often use the words of a song or even a melody to speak to us. Years ago God told me that I should never dance with another person, but only dance before Him in worship. He often speaks to me through the Holy Spirit who is so active during worship times.

5. Through prophecy

If you have had a word spoken over you and it is of God, it will always come true. It doesn't matter how far-fetched it seems, or how hard it may be to believe. If its origin is of God it will be accomplished.

6. Through Jesus

Often when we come to the cross and confess both our sinfulness and His goodness and grace, this speaks to us. If we look at the names of Jesus and what they mean for us in any given situation, we can start living in the truth of those names and share testimony with one another.

7. Through our hearts
Psalm 119:11 says:

> *"I have hidden your word in my heart that I might not sin against you."*   NIV

If we read and take in God's word it will come back to us at times when we need it. The Bible encourages us to hold the word before us so that we do not forget what it says. Orthodox Jewish men still wear a small leather box (or Phylactery) on the left arm and head containing four portions of Old Testament Scripture that remind them of the power of God's word. But we who have the Spirit of God within us need no such outward sign. We have all we need within us by His power.

Logos not logic

Some people use the word of God inappropriately. Maybe you have had a word spoken over you that was simply not of God. When I was younger, a lady came to my Dad and said that I had a gift of preaching and that my Dad should pay for me to go to Bible college. But my Dad very wisely said, "Until God tells my son that, I won't do a thing!" (My Dad was great!) I wasn't ever meant to go to Bible college. God said it would ruin me and I would ruin it! (I think He was more worried about the impact I would have on the Bible College if I'm honest!). This lady could see a gift in me, but she used human logic to take her from A to B.

How often do we do the same thing? It's easily done, isn't it?

Over the years some very wise people have offered me jobs at other churches. They have said things like, "We prayed about this and feel you should go and minister in Cardiff."

I have responded by saying, "You haven't prayed about it and the answer is no!"

Affronted, they have asked me, "How can you say that I haven't even prayed about it?"

But you see it's simple. God unequivocally told me I was going to stay in Solihull until I die. So I knew they hadn't really prayed and heard from Him. They had applied "logic" but not "Logos" to the situation.

Perhaps you need some prayer to be set free from a false word that has been binding you? Perhaps someone told you that you would get married or have a baby and it hasn't happened for you? You are therefore full of doubt and now mistrust the word of God because that dream hasn't materialised. I am not judging the person who told you that. They may well have said it innocently or from a motive of deep love for you. But I would strongly encourage you to receive some prayer to release you from any power that false promise has had over your life.

We want the best for people, but our route to that isn't always the route God wants to take. He sometimes goes in a different direction because He wants to teach us something. Look at the story of Joseph for example: God takes him through all sorts of trials before He fulfils the early dreams that he had.

So whose word do you listen to? Whose report will you believe today? God does not speak lies. He does not deal in falsehood. He is the same yesterday, today and forever. What he said yesterday will still be true today. His word NEVER fails!

What has God spoken over you in recent days?

What promises are you waiting on?

You can get excited again today that His word will be accomplished in you! Amen.

Thinking it through:

"We do not read the Bible the way it is; we read it the way we are."—Evelyn Uyemura

- ◊ How do you feel about God's word?
- ◊ Do you know it well and handle it effectively or do you often feel unsure about its meaning?
- ◊ Look back at the characteristics of God's word we have listed and at the different ways people can hear from God. How many of those do you feel God has used to speak to you?
- ◊ In what ways would you like to hear from God more?

Maybe you could sum up your thoughts and feelings in a prayer now, seeking God to be the word of life that you need in your heart right now.

CHAPTER 4
Abundant Life

What's the point?

Alan Bennett said that life is like a tin of sardines: we're all of us looking for the key. For many people, the purpose of life and death is a mystery that cannot be understood. We hear many people asking the question, "What's the point of it all?" Yet, God has promised us in His Word *abundant life*. As God's representatives on earth, we must therefore arm ourselves with the truths we find in Scripture and understand that the abundant life Jesus promises us *is available*, in this life and the next.

The uniqueness of human life is dramatised in the actions of both birth and death. A parent will stand amazed when a new baby is born, holding the tiny child, aware that here is a fresh start, a new life, a special individual. Death too can hold similar amazement. It doesn't matter how "ready" we are for someone to die, the finality of it often takes us by surprise. I find that even seasoned medical professionals, confronted with death every day, still weep and find they have no words to share with grieving families.

Solomon, reputed to be the wisest man in the Bible, said:

"He has also set eternity in the hearts of men; yet they cannot fathom what God has done from beginning to end."

(Ecclesiastes 3:11 NIV)

Jesus' mission was to bring abundant life

In John 10:10 Jesus explains His reason for coming to earth:

"I have come that they may have life, and that they may have it more abundantly."

(NKJV)

His eternal plan from the first, was to give us life in all its fullness and joy. Later in John 11:25 Jesus says,

"I am the resurrection and the life. He who believes in Me, though he may die, he shall live."

Incredibly, Jesus chose to become like us so that we could become like Him again. Here lies the key to living abundantly.

Death trap

Many of us living today just do not expect death. Advancements in medicine mean that very few of us die young. If you go back to my parents' childhood, *most* families had children who never reached maturity. In fact, there was a time in our nation when the average life expectancy was sixty years.

Would you believe that four hundred years ago, in the UK, if you reached the age of thirty-two you were considered an "old person"?

Recently I attended a funeral at the local crematorium and one of the staff there said to me, "It's a bit quiet today. We're not getting so many deaths at the moment."

"Why's that?" I asked, a bit surprised.

"People are just living longer," he responded.

If medical science reaches the point where it is possible to replace a person's heart, lungs and kidneys, then it could be possible for people to live well beyond one hundred years. Then, if somebody dies at eighty they'll be considered young! Imagine that!

But this advancement in age has very little to do with God. When some people do not reach what we consider to be a "ripe old age" we begin to look for reasons and try to come up with formulas or diagnoses to which we can accredit blame. Christians fall into this trap just as much as unbelievers. Some Christians even blame generational curses for the premature end of a life, but I believe this is a dangerous trap to fall into. I can't believe that God would let somebody die because four generations ago an ancestor of his sinned against Him in some way. As believers we are redeemed and set free by the cross of Jesus Christ and we can trust in His redemptive power.

The Church frequently finds itself confused about such issues. Why is this? I believe it is because so many today have a flawed spiritual understanding of what Jesus meant by abundant life.

In Ephesians, Paul teaches us that true life is nothing to do with breath; it's to do with our spirits.

"As for you, you were dead in your transgressions and sins, in which you used to live when you followed the ways of this world and of the ruler of the kingdom of the air, the spirit who is now at work in those who are disobedient. All of us also lived

among them at one time, gratifying the cravings of our sinful nature and following its desires and thoughts. Like the rest, we were by nature objects of wrath. But because of his great love for us, God, who is rich in mercy, made us alive with Christ even when we were dead in transgressions—it is by grace you have been saved. And God raised us up with Christ and seated us with him in the heavenly realms in Christ Jesus, in order that in the coming ages he might show the incomparable riches of his grace, expressed in his kindness to us in Christ Jesus. For it is by grace you have been saved, through faith—and this not from yourselves, it is the gift of God— not by works, so that no one can boast. For we are God's workmanship, created in Christ Jesus to do good works, which God prepared in advance for us to do."

(Ephesians 2:1-10 NIV)

Clearly we are not excluded from the process of death, but we are promised a life afterwards with God forever. What does this promise mean to us this side of death, and what will it mean in eternity? To grasp this we need to look at what abundant life really looks like.

Abundant life is characterised by being:

a) Full of light
John 8:12 says,

> *"I am the light of the world. He who follows Me shall not walk in darkness, but have the light of life."*
>
> NKJV

When we live the way we are intended to, we walk not in darkness, despair or confusion, but in light, joy and order. Abundant life like this is full of hope. We know who we are following and sense both His purpose and direction.

b) *Satisfying*
John 6:35 says,

> "I am the bread of life. He who comes to Me shall never hunger, and he who believes in Me shall never thirst."　　　　　　　　　　　　　　NKJV

If we have life as God wants it, we won't be hungering or thirsting after other things. Abundant life promises to quell our appetite and quench our thirst. It gives us all we need and satisfies our deepest longings.

c) *Eternal*
John 6:47-48 says,

> "I say to you, he who believes in Me has everlasting life. I am the bread of life."　　　　　　　　NKJV

Jesus describes Himself as the Living Bread that came down from heaven. If anyone eats of this bread, he will live forever. This promise does not have a sell-by date! It will not spoil or "go off". The bread that Jesus gives us is for all time.

We need to remember that all these characteristics of abundant life are based on the character of Jesus Himself. He says in each of these three examples, "I am ..." not, "I was" or "I will be"! Our abundant life is so life-giving because of the "I Am-ness" of the One giving it to us!

The Spiritual Life

John 3:16 says,

> *"For God so loved the world that He gave His only begotten Son, that whoever believes in Him should not perish but have everlasting life."* NKJV

In this well known verse John describes the options open to all humankind as we consider the offer of life that God places before us. We can either *perish* or accept His gift of *everlasting life*. "Perishing" here actually means "diminished" – a life that is diminished of purpose and of destiny. In fact, it's the exact opposite of everything that everlasting life contains.

The Bible makes it clear to us all that there are two types of life, physical and spiritual:

1. Physical
We all have a physical life in our bodies that we try to prolong. We exercise, feed and clothe ourselves. We build human relationships and store human knowledge in our minds. To the non-Christian, the humanist, this is the one certainty of life. They see the body as a natural, temporal, disease-attracting, age-diminishing carcass that has evolved over millions of years from primitive matter, filled with self-created ambition and fantasies that will one day re-engage with the elements, with no future destiny.

2. Spiritual
Despite the humanist view, most philosophies in this world, Buddhism, Shintoism, Islam, Sikhism and Hinduism, recognise that the human life in its physical aspect is just breath which provides transport for the true man, which is his *spirit*.

When an artist paints, he's putting on canvas that which is in his heart. When a poet writes, he is pouring onto paper that which is in his heart. God, the source of all life, is spirit, not flesh. So, when God made the earth, He was creating it from that which was in His heart. The creation of life was a tangible revelation of what God was, and is, spiritually. When God breathed into man he became a living soul, made in the image of God Himself.

That's what separates us from monkeys! We may have similar DNA, the same type of primitive functions and almost the same look, some of us! But the thing that makes us different, is not the missing link of evolution, but the missing implantation of the Holy Spirit. God breathed into you and me and we became a living soul. No animal has that incredible privilege and blessing.

The spiritual life can be dissected into three parts: abundant life, eternal life and resurrected life.

Abundant Life

If we look at John 10:10 again:

> *"I have come that they may have life, and that they may have it more abundantly"*

We see that the word abundantly here means "excessively, generously and lavishly".

We are promised an abundant life of blessing. Sometimes we say, "God's got me a good job ... He's put food on my table ... He's healed my body." Yes, God does do these things because He says, "I would that you prosper as your soul prospers" (paraphrased from Mark 10:30).

But if we are honest, this isn't always our experience, is it?

Sometimes we can feel like we are lurching from disaster to disaster and we become cynical with God, thinking, "Why has God let me down? Why has He not kept His promises to me?"

In response God says to us, "I have, but I don't talk about life as you talk about life."

The trouble is that we don't often see things in the *spirit*, we only see things in the flesh. God brings Himself down to our level to talk flesh, but He is not flesh. Neither are we in our essence! We are spirit encased in flesh. If we don't understand this we're never going to enjoy an abundant spiritual life.

Abundant life isn't a life without adversity or challenge, it is a life that embraces every circumstance, aware that God is never working from a "Plan B" mentality. There is a heart of lavish love behind every thought and action of our Heavenly Father. His abundant life is open to all of us!

Eternal Life

What do we believe eternal life to be? There are only three references to eternity in the Old Testament, yet forty-seven in the New. Why is this? It's because Jesus Himself was that life. He was abundant life, He was eternal life, He is resurrected life.

Jesus brought the reality of eternity to humanity.

> "...as You have given Him authority over all flesh, that He should give eternal life to as many as You have given Him. And this is eternal life, that they may know You, the only true God, and Jesus Christ whom You have sent."
>
> (John 17:2-4 NKJV)

In Deuteronomy it says this:

> *"The eternal God is your refuge,*
> *And underneath are the everlasting arms;*
> *He will thrust out the enemy from before you,*
> *And will say, 'Destroy!'"*
>
> (Deuteronomy 33:27 NKJV)

You may find it hard to believe that there is an eternity waiting for you, where God has eternal and everlasting arms as your refuge. But this is what the Bible says! It clearly teaches us that eternity is not some kind of wishful thinking that makes death more palatable, but a solid truth, a certainty.

Resurrection life

At times in the New Testament it speaks of the "resurrection of the dead". Matthew 22:30 says

> *"For in the resurrection they neither marry nor are given in marriage, but are like angels of God in heaven."*
>
> NKJV

This tells us that the way in which God has structured Heaven is different from earth. Relationships take on a new slant and even how we look will change too. This is obviously quite a difficult concept to get our heads around, isn't it? But think about this: when you look at a kitten you can see it's a small cat, but when you look at a butterfly it's amazing to remember that it didn't come from another butterfly, but from a little bug that crawls! This is just like we are before we go into eternity with God. We enter eternity in a different state from the way we entered the world. Romans 6:5 says,

> *"For if we have been united together in the likeness of His death, certainly we also shall be in the likeness of His resurrection."*   NKJV

This scripture reveals the truth that we will take on a different "resurrection" likeness.

John 11:25 says,

> *"I am the resurrection and the life. He who believes in Me, though he may die, he shall live."*   NKJV

So we will die a physical death, but we are promised that we shall live again. I am so excited about this! When I die and my body is put into the ground, or into the furnace and the ashes are scattered, when man won't remember me any more, Christ remembers me! He will say the word and the trumpet will sound and the dead in Christ shall rise! Graves will be opened! We have got a really exciting end in Christ. We aren't going to decompose, we're going to be made new and alive with Him!

Assurance of abundant life

These three truths about life don't mean that our experience of death is any less painful or sad. Yes, we weep and grieve for those we've lost, that is right and proper and it's also how Jesus reacted when His friend Lazarus died (John 11). We don't understand sudden death and we don't have a clue why the good sometimes die young and the bad die old. But do you know, if we did understand this we wouldn't need faith, we'd only need knowledge! My faith is that I love Jesus. He's done enough for me to realise that He doesn't slip up, even when I don't understand Him.

None of us knows how long we've got. Some of us might not reach the end of this year ourselves. We just don't know. But if we know where we're going, we have that beautiful guarantee that the old hymn talks about:

"Blessed assurance, Jesus is mine!
Oh, what a foretaste of glory divine!
Heir of salvation, purchase of God,
Born of His Spirit, washed in His blood."

Francis J Crosby, 1873

Thinking it through:

James Dean is quoted as having said, "Dream as if you'll live forever, live as if you'll die today."

◊ How do you feel about your life now? Do you feel as though you are truly living or are you merely existing?
◊ Does your life have the hallmarks of an abundant life? Is it full of light, does it satisfy you and are you sure of your own eternal destiny?
◊ What do you think you need to do, pray or think about in order to make your life what God wants it to be?

CHAPTER 5
Sanctification: The Power of the Spiritual Life

What is Sanctification?

There are only five references to sanctification in the Bible, all in the New Testament. 1 Corinthians 1:30 (NASB) says,

> "But by His doing you are in Christ Jesus, who became to us wisdom from God, and righteousness and sanctification, and redemption,"

2 Corinthians 7:1 (NASB) says,

> "Therefore, having these promises, beloved, let us cleanse ourselves from all defilement of flesh and spirit, perfecting holiness in the fear of God."

Sanctification isn't just some mysterious theological word that scholars and preachers need to understand and practise. Neither is it about playing the part of the "religious person" to look good in front of others. As J.C. Ryle said:

"I declare I know of no state of soul more dangerous than to imagine we are born again and sanctified by the Holy Ghost, because we have picked up a few religious feelings."

Being sanctified is the practical outworking of God's *Holy* Spirit in our lives. It is available for all believers, those at the beginning and those nearer the end of their journey on earth.

The word "defilement" used in the passage above, is also translated in other versions as "filthiness, pollution and contamination". Not the kind of words we like to read in association with ourselves! We like to think of ourselves as forgiven, free and spiritually clean, don't we? But there is a process involved. Those things do not just "happen". We do not achieve or retain such spiritual cleansing immediately.

When Charles Wesley talked about "entire sanctification", he did not mean we would ever reach sinless perfection. We will never get to that point this side of heaven. But he believed that we can get to a point when we don't *have* to sin.

Sanctification is the act of being set apart and the process of being made holy on the inside, so that this can be seen on the outside. It is not about the *appearance* of goodness, but about the *experience* of goodness. It is, in a sense, having a spiritual shower everyday on the inside. This cannot be done by human effort alone. We need the transforming power of the Holy Spirit at work in us to achieve what He wants for our lives.

Sanctification is therefore our reaction to the action of the Holy Spirit. He changes both our character and our lifestyle. Our job is to submit and lay down those things that so easily hinder us. We need to turn away from the paths of unrighteousness and choose to walk closely with Him.

Sanctification: call to holiness

Roman Catholic nuns wear a wedding ring because they believe they are betrothed to Christ. An engagement or a wedding ring is supposed to be a sign that says, "Keep off, I'm spoken for."

In a sense every Christian wears such an "engagement" ring because we are all betrothed to, and set apart for, Christ. We are the bride and He is the groom. No man wants to marry "damaged goods". Nor does Jesus.

Paul describes the relationship of marriage in Ephesians 5:25-27 (NIV) like this:

> *"Husbands, love your wives, just as Christ loved the church and gave himself up for her to make her holy, cleansing her by the washing with water through the word, and to present her to himself as a radiant church, without stain or wrinkle or any other blemish, but holy and blameless."*

Christ is coming back for a bride without spot or wrinkle, a partner who is "holy and blameless" before Him. Spots, as we know, are often a sign of immaturity, just as wrinkles are a sign of old age. He doesn't want us unready for the relationship, or past our prime. He's looking for a people who are clean, pure and prepared for Him.

We are all called to live a holy life. Think for a minute about the 10 commandments. How many would you allow me to break as a pastor? I hope your answer is "none"! I need to live a righteous and sanctified life, especially because I am called to lead others.

I don't expect anyone on the leadership team of our church to commit adultery, to lust, to covet other people's things, to have any other gods, to blaspheme or swear. I don't expect them to murder or kill or lie. I expect them to be accountable to the call to holiness!

Sanctification: surrender to the Spirit

John Wesley talks about his brother Charles saying to him, "Have you been sanctified since you've believed?" John's reaction was, "I've never heard of this sanctification …"

A few weeks later in his journal he says, "Today, I received my sanctification." He talks about preaching saying that the people fell to the floor groaning, having received their justification and their sanctification at the same time. We would say they had been "born again" and "filled with the Spirit".

John Wesley's testimony is that he didn't reach a state of sanctification until he was filled with Holy Spirit. Only *He* has the power to break the power of sin and set the prisoner free. The more of the Spirit we have inside us, the cleaner and more sanctified we become.

Sanctification: available for all

We are so blessed that God doesn't look at us and think, "There's no hope here! I can't work on this person. They are a complete mess."

> *"For consider your calling, brethren, that there were not many wise according to the flesh, not many mighty, not many noble; but God has chosen the foolish things of the world to shame the wise, and God has chosen the weak things of the world to shame the things which are strong, and the base things of the world and the despised God has chosen, the things that are not, so that He may nullify the things that are, so that no man may boast before God. But by His doing you are in Christ Jesus, who became to us wisdom from God, and righteousness and sanctification, and redemption,"*
> (1 Corinthians 1:26-30 NASB)

Paul shows here that salvation is all about the grace of God, not the graft of man. Look at what He does:

1. God takes the foolish things of this world.
In comparison to God, we are, all of us, foolish. We may be wise in our own eyes, but compared to heavenly wisdom, we speak rubbish! But the good news is that God takes us in our foolishness and somehow uses us to shame the wise. He is not worried about the quality of the raw material. He just looks through us and is able to see His Son. "By His doing, we are in Christ." We need no other letter after our name or information on our CV than that!

2. God takes the weak things of this world.
God chooses us in our weakness and frailty to shame things that are strong. Do you sometimes feel weak and worthless? Do you look at your life and wonder why God loves you? Do you struggle to believe you were worth dying for? Join the club! Paul explains here that all of us are weak, but this is how God likes it. He takes the things that are not what they could be and turns them into what they should be. He takes you and me and gives us the gift and the grace of sanctification. Praise Him!

3. God takes the base and despised things.
Have you ever felt ashamed or despised by others? We have all been in a place like that, where we feel others look down on us. But God uses that for His purposes. Why does He do this? If you were collecting a group of people together that you wanted to change the world, would you start with you? Maybe you wouldn't, but God does. He starts with you and me in our baseness and frailty so that none of us can boast.

An eminent surgeon may deliver a diagnosis to a patient and say he can do nothing. But our God can use the simplest person to pray in faith and see that same person healed. It is baffling but true that our salvation and sanctification is an act of God, and God alone. It does not depend on the experiences and qualities we possess. It's a demonstration of His love and mercy; it's a fulfilment of His promises and it's a revelation of His powerful grace.

Sanctification: physically and sexually

The Bible is very clear that a Christian should not be living a life of sexual misconduct. If adultery, fornication and homosexuality are active then there cannot be sanctification:

> *"For this is the will of God, your sanctification: that you should abstain from sexual immorality; that each of you should know how to possess his own vessel in sanctification and honour."*
>
> (1 Thessalonians 4:3-4 NKJV)

Paul is speaking here of sanctification in respect to sexual practices. The act of human lust is not condoned as being the natural, created, hormonal drive. Being sanctified means being physically and sexually pure. The act of sex is, in biblical teaching, consummation: the act of completion, perfection and fulfilment within marriage.

Many Christians today, and especially leaders, have rejected this truth for a life of sexual promiscuity, believing that sanctification can come by ministry and gift rather than by character and integrity. But what we do in the flesh has huge effects on our spiritual health as well as our physical wellbeing. Paul, in verse 4, speaks about us learning how to control the lust of the flesh. He doesn't say that we won't struggle with lust, but that we must learn how to restrain it. This is one of the biggest driving forces that robs people of sanctification.

> *"But we are bound to give thanks to God always for you, brethren beloved by the Lord, because God from the beginning chose you for salvation through sanctification by the Spirit and belief in the truth."*
> (2 Thessalonians 2:13 NKJV)

Sanctification comes by believing truth. If you believe you can be sexually promiscuous and stay sanctified, you're believing a lie! God expects our sexual lives to be under sanctification because it is symbolic of His relationship with the Church.

My old life, in football, was often a struggle. In the 21 years I worked in that world, I could have slept with many young women because I had both the wealth and the status. The footballers, managers and promoters had a constant stream of women who were prepared to sleep with them. Amazingly beautiful women would also chat me up. It's easy to see how and why footballers have affairs.

But it's not confined to the world of football. On one occasion a woman solicited me as she walked out of church one day. She had a lovely figure, legs up to her ears and was incredibly attractive. She turned to me and said: "If you were single, what I could do for you!" It's easy to fall for a line like that! Your ego goes right through the ceiling because you know that when you go home, your wife will probably not be saying stuff like that to you. She may sit and moan at you about how long you preached for and, because of it, now the dinner is ruined!

We need to be real about the problems and struggles we face. Then maybe we will have fewer leaders falling into sin. But how do we take care not to fall in the first place?

Sanctification: avoiding temptation

To live a life of sanctification involves an act of the will. It wasn't easy for me to walk away from a highly lucrative job in football, but I knew where my sanctified life lay. Twenty years ago I was offered an unbelievably high salary to become a conference evangelist and TV preacher in America. That large amount of money, plus the exposure it would bring, made it all very tempting. But it was not what God was calling me to do. I was reminded of the words of the old hymn:

> *"Turn your eyes upon Jesus,*
> *look full in His wonderful face,*
> *and the things of the earth will grow strangely dim*
> *in the light of His glory and grace."*
>
> *(Helen H. Lemmel)*

We need to be aware that temptation isn't always adultery or something obviously evil. It can be success in ministry, an exclusive relationship, a new job. It can be subtle things that take us away from our "first love" – our calling.

I am called to be the pastor of my church in Solihull until the day I die. That's my bride; that's the image of Christ in me. But I sometimes doubt it and find myself open to the temptations of the flesh. For this reason, I find it helpful to surround myself with people to whom I can be accountable. Wherever I travel and wherever I go to speak I take someone with me.

Having someone by my side means it's harder to fall. I won't fall asleep when I'm driving; I won't be tempted to watch something unhelpful or ungodly on TV; I won't be in a situation where I could be alone with someone trying to lure me into sin. One of the reasons I never drink is because I can easily become addicted. If I eat chocolate, I down the whole lot! I have that kind of personality. I know myself well and know what I need to do to stay safe and clean. What about you? How well do you know the things that trigger temptation in you? In my experience as a pastor, it helps to know the things that make us weak, so that we can avoid them.

Sanctification: surrounding yourself with godly people

I hope that we all know people who encourage and support us. But we are also likely to know others who can easily lead us into bad habits. Maybe you are in a relationship with a friend who causes you to swear, or spend your money recklessly. Perhaps you struggle with someone flirting with you. All of us impact those around us for good or ill. We are also influenced by other people, more than we care to admit.

I'm very cautious about who I trust to come into my life. I am also, in a church context, careful about who I allow to lay hands on me. That's why I don't do what some churches do and say, "Just turn around to someone and place your hands on them…". I believe that something of our spirit is passed on when we pray for others. If you've got an adulterous, cheating, pornographic, drunken slob standing by the side of you and he puts his hands on you, do you really want any of that spirit? Do you want a gossip to put their hands on you? No! Now, I know I'm certainly not perfect but I do say, "God forgive me. Don't let me put anything on these people that isn't clean."

We should take care who we surround ourselves with and put a stop to any relationship or friendship that compromises a life of sanctification. This does not mean we have to live in a monastery and wear a habit! But we have to submit ourselves to the will of God.

Sanctification: never off duty

We can't choose to be holy one day and sinful the next. I was saying to some leaders the other day that pastors don't have private lives. Whatever statement we make in public, on television, on the radio, on Facebook or anywhere else, is not coming from an individual, it's coming from a leader in the Church of Christ. But it's not just leaders who have this calling. When we call ourselves Christian, we are aligning ourselves with the character and name of the risen Christ. Our righteousness and sanctification must always be ready to be shown at any moment.

You're always a Christian, not just when it suits you. This is a lifetime's journey. If we're going to touch the world and heal the sick, if one day we're going to raise the dead, then it's got to come from people who are sold out to purity of heart and the purity of God. People who want to be filled with the Holy Spirit. Will we become sinless? No. Will we learn to sin less? Yes. Will our character change? It will. Will our character grow? Yes it will. Will people begin to see Christ in us? You bet!

Recently, a man in our church died of pneumonia resulting from leukaemia. He said to me, with tears running down his face, "I've been a hypocrite for many years. How can I belong to a great church, hear great sermons, put a minimal amount in the offering, play my trumpet and just let life go by?"

He had everything a man could desire: a stunning wife who was his best friend as well as his lover, a beautiful child and a great job in the Police Force. But he knew that he was living a lie. Over the 16 months of his illness, he changed totally. He witnessed to the Chief Constable and to all who came in to visit him. He avidly read the Bible and the truths of it began to pour into his heart. I watched the Holy Spirit begin to sanctify him. He learnt that if God was going to take him he could do nothing about it but accept it and make himself ready.

Once, when I shared one Sunday about the apostle James speaking about hypocrites, a very influential person emailed me the next day and said, "Thank you. I am also a hypocrite and it's time I did something about it."

Do you need to say that today? Do you sometimes allow yourself "off duty" days when you slip into bad habits? If I filmed you today, right now, focused the camera on you and relayed it to your work colleagues tomorrow, would they be shocked to see you even reading this? Would they be surprised after what they know about you? What about your neighbours, your uncles and aunts, brothers and sisters? Would they be shocked to see you going to church at all?

Sanctification: living in the knowledge we are loved and chosen

Sanctification is not about living a life of rules and regulations. It is being set free to enjoy all the goodness of God set out for us in Christ. When we understand this we can rejoice and give thanks to God for who He is and how He is at work in our lives. There are some beautiful truths we can hold on to:

1. We are loved
God's sanctification is only available to us because of His deep love for us. Without this love and security we would never be made acceptable in His sight.

In John 3:16 we read the familiar words that God,

> *"So loved the world that He gave ...".*

The first commandment and the new commandment is all about love. It is easy to set yourself apart and honour someone who loves you that much. Those of you who are happily married can relate to this. On your wedding day it was not a chore to walk up the aisle and say "I do." You willingly and gladly went and you would do it again! Why? Simply because of the security of loving and being loved.

2. We are chosen from the beginning for salvation
We're a Royal Priesthood, a holy nation. Psalm 132:13 says that the Lord has chosen Zion. Psalm 135 says that the Lord has chosen Jacob. John 15:16 says,

> *"You did not choose Me, but I chose you."*

Imagine sitting in a beautiful restaurant. When you choose something from the menu, you actively seek it out. You ask for it by name. You look for it and decide you want it. This is what God has done with us. He has chosen us from the beginning for His sanctification.

Our lives are not accidents. They are part of His plan.

> *"... according to the foreknowledge of God the Father, in sanctification of the Spirit, for obedience and sprinkling of the blood of Jesus Christ: Grace to you and peace be multiplied."*
> (1 Peter 1:2 NKJV)

Notice it says foreknowledge and not predestined. God loved us before the very foundations of the earth. The Father loved us, the Holy Spirit revealed it to us and Jesus sealed it in His blood!

What a God we serve!

Thinking it through:

"God loves you just the way you are, but he refuses to leave you that way."

Max Lucado

◊ What areas of your life do you feel the Holy Spirit has been highlighting for you as you have read this?
◊ Are there any relationships or patterns of behaviour that you need to submit afresh to God for His cleansing and help?
◊ In what ways do you feel challenged to live a more sanctified life?

Why not take some time now to write your own prayer of thanksgiving to God and ask the Holy Spirit to dwell in you and carry on the process of making you holy.

Chapter 6

The Fulfilment of Forgiveness

"To forgive is to set a prisoner free and discover that the prisoner was you."

—*Lewis B Smedes*

What is forgiveness?

Forgiveness is an issue that we all know about, but few of us actually ever live in – and I'm including Christians, leaders and pastors in this statement! The trouble is that we find ways to justify why we shouldn't or can't forgive. Sixty years on, people who served in the war will say, "I will not buy a car made by *those* people. How can I forgive them after what they did to my friends?"

In the natural I can understand that, but forgiveness is not natural, it is utterly of God. Forgiveness does not condone wrongdoing. It never has done. By forgiving someone we are not "letting them off" or showing weakness. Forgiveness is a sign of huge strength. Someone who can live in forgiveness is a complete and whole person open to the blessing and favour of God.

I meet people all the time who are eaten up with bitterness due to unforgiveness in their lives. Holding onto a grudge is a curse to the soul and a confusion to the mind. It is exhausting to maintain and can ruin whole lives. But the power of forgiveness changes lives, sets people free and even causes physical changes in us.

Jesus taught forgiveness

The passage of Luke 11 is one of the most quoted scriptures in the Bible and is what's commonly called "The Lord's Prayer". Jesus actually said here, "Say this …" That's good enough for me! He didn't say, "It's figurative" or "It's not really a prayer, it's a guide." If we pray it as Jesus meant us to, I honestly believe we will never be the same again. Everything we need to pray about forgiveness is contained in this short passage.

This prayer was given as an answer to the question, "Teach us to pray." The disciples had seen and heard Jesus pray, but then looked at themselves and said, "We haven't got a clue how to pray like that. Teach us!" There was an emptiness in them and in their communication with God. This was not really their fault. Until Jesus came, prayers were never said directly to God, people always went through a priest. When people died, there were qualified mourners who would weep and, if they got paid more, they'd cry louder! There were also "professional pray-ers". But Jesus is opening up a whole new possibility of relationship with the Father in this prayer. We need to recognise some truths about Him first.

Recognition of His Fatherhood

> "He said to them, "When you pray, say: 'Father, hallowed be your name, your kingdom come.'"
>
> (Luke 11:2 NIV)

Before Jesus came, God's people never had real intimacy with Him. They were not even allowed to pronounce His name. But here, Jesus says, "You can now address Him as 'My Father'." This was completely revolutionary for those listening. What I love about Jesus is that He doesn't say, "Well, one day you can call Him Father." This is good news for us: we haven't got to wait; we haven't got to go through a process, or complete a course or become a priest. We can speak to Him directly as we would to our own father. It's no wonder that some of the Pharisees and the Sadducees wanted to kill Him! What He was saying was utterly blasphemous in their understanding. Here was Jesus, telling people to address God as "Abba", the most intimate expression of all meaning "Daddy"!

I wonder if you'd like a personal relationship like that with God? I would. In fact, that's my daily quest. Living a life of forgiveness starts with the recognition of God's fatherhood. Until we know Him as our Father, we cannot know Him as our forgiver and then choose to forgive others.

Recognition of His Will

Jesus teaches us to say, "Your will be done." Of course, once we do this we're under submission. This means that if God asks us to forgive someone, we need to do it! We all struggle with handing over control of our lives in this way. We want to be in charge. I can remember when God led me to Solihull.

If I am honest, I did not go gladly at first. I wanted to be an evangelist, not a pastor. Sometimes it's not easy to surrender to God, but it is always the best road for us to travel. I have seen endless blessing and forgiveness in my own life because I chose to submit to the will of God in this way.

Recognition of His Authority

> *"And He said to them, When you pray, say: Our Father Who is in heaven, hallowed be Your name, Your kingdom come. Your will be done, held holy and revered, on earth as it is in heaven."*
>
> (Luke 11:2-3 Amplified Bible)

In order to live lives of forgiveness we also need to understand God's authority "on earth, as in heaven". Unless we know this, we cannot fully understand what He's asking us to do. In this prayer, Jesus tells us who God is and that His name is *hallowed* or Holy – meaning set apart and unique.

Jesus shares with us the reality of a coming kingdom. We tend to live our lives as if God's on "catch up": "Oh God, I've got a problem and I know You don't know anything about it, but if you don't sort it out by tomorrow, it'll be too late." God is not trying His best to keep up with us; His kingdom is here and it is also coming. His reign is ahead as well as in the present. I wish we were all as excited about God's kingdom coming, as children are about Father Christmas! Jesus is coming back for those who are looking for His appearing. But many of us today don't expect or preach much about Jesus returning. We are too busy playing church!

Recognition of the path of forgiveness

> *"And forgive us our sins, for we ourselves also forgive everyone who is indebted to us, who has offended us or done us wrong."*
>
> (Luke 11:4 Amplified Bible)

This part of the scripture is very challenging. So far, the prayer has recognised God as a Father in charge, with a coming kingdom. It has asked of Him that He would supply our food, both spiritual and physical. Now Jesus comes to something WE have to do. This is the only part of the prayer that is conditional. Jesus is saying, "Forgive us our sins *only* to the level that we forgive others." If you are sitting there reading this with unforgiveness in your life, God is speaking to you right now! Forgiveness is not what we say, it's how we live. Do you realise that if you are withholding forgiveness towards someone who has wronged you, you have shut off the road by which God can forgive you? That's what it says!

Matthew 6, Matthew's recording of the Lord's Prayer, goes further:

> *"For if you forgive men their trespasses, your heavenly Father will also forgive you. But if you do not forgive men their trespasses, neither will your Father forgive your trespasses."*
>
> (Matthew 6:14-15 NKJV)

Unforgiveness can look like this. You can go for prayer every week and never feel free. You can seek God for emotional or physical healing and never see a breakthrough. You can try to make relationships but always be suspicious and guarded with others. You can rehearse over and over in your mind the things said and done to you until they are blown out of all proportion. You can make comments to others that will destroy reputations. Does this sound familiar to you?

What is the result of all of these things? God will stop speaking to you and blessing you.

The word forgive means to "lay it on one side". Have you ever said to someone, "Just let it go, will you?" That's forgiveness. It means forsake it, leave it and omit it from your vocabulary, your mind and your heart.

God is forgiving by nature. In Exodus 34:6 (NIV) it says, He is *"slow to anger"*. It's not that He does not get angry, but that He's slow to become that way. He is,

> *"... abounding in love and faithfulness, maintaining love to thousands, and forgiving wickedness, rebellion and sin."*

It's true that society cannot cope with those who forgive. I know lots of Christians who say, "Look what's happened to you! How can you forgive people when they've done that to you?" I hear Christians say that to other Christians! But I believe that there is no place in Christianity for unforgiveness.

My own journey to forgiveness

I find it hard now to believe that I used to be such a venomous man, but it's true. In the very old days I'd even attack my enemies physically. No one wanted to cross me. Not many people would take me on for an argument because I was so quick. I could cut people dead with my comments. I didn't mind how long I waited to do it either. Like an elephant, I never forgot an offence against me and I always paid the person back.

But when the forgiveness of Christ entered my world, everything changed. It wasn't that people stopped hurting me, far from it! In fact most of the people who have sought to do the most damage to me over the years have been brothers and sisters in Christ. But I can say, as God is my judge, I cannot think of anybody I have any unforgiveness over. It's the reason I'm still pastor of my church while many of my friends have left the ministry. They've got bitterness and unforgiveness in their hearts. I haven't.

I'm not boasting, this is normal Christian living. Have people hurt me? You'd better believe it. Have they caused me to cry? Yes. Have they betrayed me? Yes. Have they misquoted me? Yes they have. Have they lied about me? Yes they have. Have they made me promises they didn't fulfil? Yes. Did I like it? No I didn't. Did it hurt me? Immensely. Did it cause me to feel ill? Yes. Have I felt violated? Yes. But did I get over it? YES!

I believe that without forgiveness we cannot call ourselves Christians. That's what makes us unique from any other faith. We do not have to go out and, if someone disagrees with us or God, kill them. We love them. This sometimes doesn't feel natural or our first response, but it is what we are called to do and how we are asked to act.

Whole churches can be decimated by unforgiveness. The spirit of offence deprives us of God's saving power. Where there is no release there is only bondage. That's why when a person comes to join our church we say, *"If you've left your previous church unrighteously or you got hurt in your last church, you have to put it right before you come here."* I will not have unforgiveness in this church. I will not have bitterness. I've seen it happen. Great ministries go, families divide, marriages crash, kids become delinquent – all because of unforgiveness.

"For Your name's sake, O LORD,
Pardon my iniquity, for it is great.
Who is the man that fears the Lord?
Him shall He teach in the way He chooses.
He himself shall dwell in prosperity,
And his descendants shall inherit the earth.
The secret of the Lord is with those who fear Him,
And He will show them His covenant.
My eyes are ever toward the Lord."

(Psalm 25:11-14 NKJV)

Look what happens when we are pardoned! God shows us His covenant. I want to be in that place where God confides in me. Don't you?

I can go to anybody now who has hurt me, anybody – in fact I met someone yesterday and put my arm around them – and say it's great to see them and mean it. They might sweat a bit and feel uncomfortable, but I don't. I just feel clean before God. Its been dealt with and it is not holding me back. Perhaps there are a number of people you need to feel like that about today?

Maybe you walk down the road and suddenly see someone diving into a shop because they don't want to bump into you? Perhaps you see someone in church or at an event that you are not at peace with, but they ignore you. Go home and pray. Release them from your hurt and anger. Sometimes you've done nothing; it's just their insecurity or fear. Forgiving as we have been forgiven has great power. You do not need to live with that having a hold on you.

The Power of Forgiveness

In Mark 2 there is the story of a man who is lowered, by his friends, through a roof. He was sick and in this case the Lord discerned that it was not lack of faith that disqualified this man from being healed, but it was lack of forgiveness:

> *Since they could not get him to Jesus because of the crowd, they made an opening in the roof above Jesus and, after digging through it, lowered the mat the paralysed man was lying on. When Jesus saw their faith, he said to the paralytic, "Son, your sins are forgiven."*
> (Mark 2:4-5 NIV)

Jesus saw not the man's faith, but the faith of his friends. What he realised the paralytic needed most was forgiveness. Perhaps the man had become bitter and twisted over his sickness; maybe he was also resentful of his friends taking him?

I can imagine him saying, "I haven't asked you to bring me here. Don't tell me there's a God or I wouldn't be lying on this stretcher now. Don't you tell me there's a good God when I was born like this."

Jesus could see that unforgiveness in this man was crippling him, both physically and emotionally.

He dealt with the root cause first. Jesus understood that unforgiveness can bring you illness and can keep you in illness.

I have seen this, rather painfully, for myself. Many years ago Reinhard Bonnke met someone suffering with illness and was going to pray for them when God told him to say, "No. You'll only be healed when David Carr prays for you." It just so happened that the person he was talking to knew and *hated* me, though they were a Christian.

Many years later Reinhard saw me and said, "How's so-and-so now?"

I said, "Sick."

He said, "What? I can't understand that. God told me distinctly that if you laid hands on them they'd be healed."

"Really?" I said.

Reinhard did not know that this person hated my guts. I never told him the story. This person could have been healed thirty or forty years ago. They have been prayed for by all the leading ministries in the world but, sadly, will take that sickness to their grave unless they deal with their unforgiveness about me.

Forgiveness has such power.

Who can forgive sins?

The teachers of the Law attacked Jesus because He forgave people. Their view was that only God can forgive in this way and accused Him of blasphemy:

> *"Why does this fellow talk like that? He's blaspheming! Who can forgive sins but God alone?"*
>
> (Mark 2:7 NIV)

Who has the power and authority to forgive sin in this way? Only God! Look at these other scriptures that show us where Jesus spoke into man's deepest need:

1. Luke 7:36 tells us the story of the woman who anointed Jesus with fragrant oil. Jesus said, "Woman don't sin any more. I forgive you." The religious leaders attacked Him because He forgave prostitutes like her. It was just not in their worldview to do the same.

2. Luke 6:37 says,

    > *"Judge not, and you shall not be judged. Condemn not, and you shall not be condemned. Forgive, and you will be forgiven."*   NKJV

Jesus is saying here, "Give and it will be given to you. With the same measure that you use, all these things will be measured back to you."

3. In Matthew 18, Peter asks Jesus: "How many times should I forgive? ... Seven?"

Why did he say seven? Under Jewish law you were required to forgive someone three times if they sinned against you, but not the fourth. So Peter was wondering how far Jesus would extend His grace. But Jesus said,

"Try four hundred and ninety times!"

Do you get the message? Jesus was saying that the forgiveness available in God is not exhaustible. It does not require a formula but a freedom.

Repentance not reprisal

The whole of Christianity is based not on reprisal but on repentance; it's not based on ferocity but forgiveness. Forgiveness is not the endorsement of the perpetrator or the perpetration, it is recognising that judgement is a divine prerogative and does not come under the remit of man. By trying to sit in judgement over someone, we challenge God's leadership and authority. There is only one who is the judge of the living and the dead.

Forgiveness breaks any control the violator has over us. I often pray, especially for those who have been abused, that God will give them the gift of forgiveness. This is the only thing that will set them free. I have met countless, women in particular, who, as small children, were violated by men. They may be in their fifties now but have never been free of the past. Unforgiveness is so powerfully active in their spirit it's as if that man abused them yesterday. They believe that to forgive him is to let him off the hook, but actually, to forgive him heals them and releases that person to be judged. If we're sitting in judgement over someone, God can't get to them. We are actually protecting them from the Almighty rather than releasing them. If you forgive, then you get healed and they get released for God to act.

How tragic that for so many years such people have not moved on. I love watching God at work in cases like this! He drives away all shame and fear. He brings deep forgiveness that sets people free.

Father forgive them...

Forgiveness breaks the control of the violator and the violation. The offence is no longer able to manifest pain, grief, unforgiveness, bitterness, anger, tears, temper, unrighteousness, suspicion, loss of trust, cynicism, gossip and living in the past. And believe me, some Christians suffer from all of that rubbish!

> *"Then Jesus said, 'Father, forgive them, for they do not know what they do."*
>
> (Luke 23:34 NKJV)

Even on the cross, Jesus implores His Father to be merciful to us. "Father! Don't do it. Forgive them because that's the reason You sent me. Don't get upset, don't wipe them out …"

I wonder if we would be here right now if Jesus had not said that? God was ready to wipe out the whole nation of Israel for building a golden calf! What do you think He was going to do to the world for killing His Son? But Jesus said, "No Dad, just remember this is the reason I came. Don't kill them; save them."

> *"Therefore, as God's chosen people, holy and dearly loved, clothe yourselves with compassion, kindness, humility, gentleness and patience. Bear with each other and forgive whatever grievances you may have against one another. Forgive as the Lord forgave you."*
>
> (Colossians 3:12-13 NIV)

We have been offered a life full and free of the pain and trauma of grudge matches and unforgiveness. What are we going to do to accept it?

Thinking it through:

"When you hold resentment towards another, you are bound to that person or condition by an emotional link that is stronger than steel. Forgiveness is the only way to dissolve that link and get free." —Catherine Ponder

◊ How do you feel about your own life in the light of reading this chapter?
◊ Is there someone who you find it hard to think about without anger or pain rising within you?
◊ What do you think God is asking of you?

You may find it helpful to talk and pray the issue through with a mature Christian whom you trust.

You may also like to use this prayer:

"Father God, I want to thank You that You will forgive my trespasses as I forgive those who trespass against me. I want to release anyone who has hurt me. Help me now to forgive them unreservedly. I set them free from my judgement, for who am I to judge?

As I forgive, I know You forgive me and that You will make up any deficit or emptiness in my life, filling it with the forgiveness Jesus brings. Amen."

Some of you have read this and know you need to write a letter or make a phone call. You may be in tears as you read these words, knowing they are just for you, as if God Himself were speaking! He is!

If the person you speak to does not accept your forgiveness, it is still dealt with in the heavenly realms. It is now their problem, not yours. Walk away because it is now between them and God. If they respond well to you, then that's a bonus, but don't expect it. You forgive, not to get anything out of it, but because it's what your King requires of you.

I pray that God releases you into His wholeness and allows you to live a life full of the power of His forgiveness and grace. Amen!

CHAPTER 7

Unspeakable Joy

Joy is normal

Why is it that we are all looking for happiness when it is both so transient and circumstantial? Happiness may come to us in different shapes and forms. A new carpet, a grandchild, the house you've always wanted or the car you're driving. Those are wonderful things, but you don't need God in order to have them – all you need are the right circumstances that "push your button". A lot of non-Christians are very happy people. I hear believers say, "Well, they'll never be *really* happy until they have been saved," but a lot of people who've never been near Christianity believe themselves to be genuinely happy and don't see any need for God. Aren't the people at your place of work happy? Don't you look at them sometimes and think they are happier than you?

Many Christians have forgotten why we should be and how to be joyful.

People frequently say to me:

"Pastor Dave, at your age you preach four or five times a week and yet you're full of joy! I don't know how you do it! How have you kept doing this week in and week out for 38 years?" My answer is always the same: *the joy of the Lord is my strength!* Some people suffer from stress, but I haven't got enough time for it. I looked in my diary the other week to try and find time for it and I couldn't! Instead I prefer to live inside God's joy.

It's not a show that I put on either. I'm not superhuman – in fact, I know I'm deficient in many areas. But I see myself as completely normal. I'm just a basic Christian. I am just trying to be the person that God expects me to be. I am not a superstar. I'm never going to be a great preacher, an outstanding pastor or a superb writer. I'm never going to be that great at anything! I'm not being modest. I look at myself according to Scripture and think I'm just about reaching normal. My job, as a pastor and a writer, is to inspire you to develop the habits of a normal Christian too.

I want to encourage you today to assess your own levels of joy. Would you describe yourself as a joyful person? When people meet you do they meet someone bubbling over with the joy of the Lord, or do they meet a person who struggles to smile behind gritted teeth and moans about everything?

The Psalmist said in Psalm 16:11,

> *"You will show me the path of life; in Your presence is fullness of joy."*   NKJV

I honestly believe that when we are in God's presence and continually surrounded with Him, we cannot help but experience "fullness of joy".

What is joy?

There are 7 words in the New Testament we translate into the word "joy". Luke alone uses these words an amazing

36 times. There are 326 occurrences of the word for joy in the New Testament and 131 are found in the 10 letters that are usually ascribed to Paul. The word joy has a root in the word *charis*, which means grace. Paul's understanding of joy is therefore rooted in his knowledge of God's favour and grace over him. That makes sense doesn't it? Unless one has known the favour of God, what is there to rejoice about? Paul speaks of joy being the product of *being in Christ*. Philippians 3:1 says,

> *"rejoice in the Lord."*
>
> NKJV

and Philippians 4:4 says,

> *"Rejoice in the Lord always. Again I will say, rejoice!"*
>
> NKJV

One of the meanings of joy is to be "exalted", in other words placed at a higher level. The whole essence of God is that He loves us so much that He wants to do something amazing for us and give us something we don't deserve. Joy, then, is the knowledge that we are being built up far above our circumstance. Joy also means to be glad and rejoice. You can't rejoice by sitting with your mouth shut. When a footballer scores a goal, his supporters and team mates rejoice. After the match they walk down the street singing, shouting, arm-in-arm, rejoicing! Joy therefore involves bodily action as well as verbal expression. Rejoicing is when everything we know and feel inwardly is proclaimed outwardly.

But how can joy be manifest in our life even when things are going badly? How can people we know still praise God even when their baby has died of cancer or they have lost their job? This is because true joy is founded in one's spirit and not one's emotions. Joy is based on something deeper and more profound than happiness and wellbeing.

Romans 5:11 says,

> *"And not only that, but we also rejoice in God through our Lord Jesus Christ, through whom we have now received the reconciliation."*   NKJV

We can break forth with joy because we, who were once alien to God, have now been brought back into relationship with Him.

Paul also speaks of how others make him rejoice. If you've got joy within you, you're grateful for people and find the good in how others treat you. Notice that Paul is honest about the lack of care given to him before, but he realises it was down to lack of opportunity, not desire.

> *"But I rejoiced in the Lord greatly that now at last your care for me has flourished again; though you surely did care, but you lacked opportunity."*
> (Philippians 4:10 NKJV)

Joy is not only just seen in the New Testament.

> *"When David was returning from the slaughter of the Philistines, the women had come out of all the cities of Israel, singing and dancing, to meet King Saul, with tambourines, with joy, and with musical instruments."*
> (1 Samuel 18:6 NKJV)

In Psalm 16:8-9, we read these amazing words that give us a clue to the source and reason for being a joyful people:

> *"I have set the LORD always before me;*
> *Because He is at my right hand I shall not be moved.*
> *Therefore my heart is glad, and my glory rejoices;*
> *My flesh also will rest in hope."*   NKJV

In this psalm we can see a clear progression, beginning with a positive choice, that leads us to joy.

1. "I have set the Lord before me" – I choose to put God first.
2. "Because He is at my right hand" – He is never far from me.
3. "I shall not be moved" – nothing will change how I act or feel.
4. "Therefore my heart is glad" – joy is my ongoing choice.
5. "My glory rejoices" – everything in me speaks of that joy.
6. "My flesh also will rest in hope" – all that I am will now be at peace.

Read that list again to yourself out loud! It's a very powerful set of truths that I want you to get into your spirit today. You see, it's no good us just going to church and saying, "Oh, I feel better now." That's just experiencing a bit of a lift. Your joy and my joy needs to be based on something more powerful than a good song or a well-preached sermon. If we are going to get through that redundancy, losing our house, that terrible bereavement or long-term illness, unspeakable heavenly joy is the only antidote.

That's where the progression I just showed you is all-important. It's not about "putting on a brave face" or acting a part; it's about *being a part* of God's plan for us. It may involve coming apart, but it won't involve falling apart.

When we have this kind of joy it is like a deeply profound peace. It is largely inexplicable. It does not depend on what is happening for us or around us. This is because the things of God are not *opposites*, they're *collectives*. Joy is not merely the opposite of sadness or despair. You can't really tell where God's joy finishes and His peace begins. The beautiful gifts of God slot together in our lives a bit like a jigsaw puzzle.

Let me tell you about an amazingly joyful man. Billy Bray was one of the early primitive Methodist preachers in Cornwall. He was a tin miner and a gambling drunk when the Holy Spirit broke through to him. He was convicted so powerfully one day that he was paralysed in the street and his wife had to drag him by his shirt back into the house. He was wonderfully born again. He built many of the little Methodist chapels in Cornwall. He worked in the mines at night and in the daytime he preached and filled every one of these chapels. He was known as "the son of the King". He was reported to have said, "If you put me in a barrel I'd shout 'Glory!' through the bung hole!"

One day his wife became very ill. The doctor came round and after a while said, "Mr Bray, I'm afraid your wife has died."

Billy went upstairs with his pit boots on to look at his wife's body and the people downstairs could hear his boots stamping.

They rushed upstairs to find him both crying and laughing, and then leaping and dancing.

Shocked, the doctor said, "Mr Bray, have you no respect for the dead?"

But Bray answered, "Have you no realisation where she is?"

This man was so full of the joy of the Holy Spirit that he could dance around the bed of his just dead wife, knowing full well that she was caught up in glory! He really knew how to be joyful!

Becoming more joyful

So what are the keys to being joyful?

Being in the Lord's presence
We read earlier David's line from Psalm 16:

> *"In your presence is fullness of joy."*
>
> NKJV

If we went to church more often, turned up for prayer meetings and spent time in His presence on a daily basis we would have more joy. In Matthew 25 part of the reward for being a good and faithful servant was to enter into the "joy of the Lord". It's a reward to live in the bliss of laughter, of dancing and making merry. Where can we find such joy? In His presence.

Being with joyful people
If we mix with a world that's negative or surround ourselves with critical people all the time, what are we going to become? It is obvious that we will take on their traits and become a more pessimistic person.

However, if we are with people who are full of joy, that is also catching! We start to become more joyful too, more able to see God's plans, even in trying circumstances. Our joy is made manifest because the Lord has revealed the path of life to us.

> *"You will show me the path of life; in Your presence is fullness of joy; at Your right hand are pleasures forevermore."*
> (Psalm 16:11 NKJV)

If we look at some of the biblical statements about joy we see lots of noise attached! Tambourines, flutes rejoicing, cymbals and shouting for joy. Nehemiah, during the rebuilding of Jerusalem, built a platform for Ezra to preach from. Rather than being sad or religious he commanded the people to eat, drink and to rejoice greatly:

> *"Do not sorrow for the joy of the LORD is your strength."*
> (Nehemiah 8:10 NKJV)

When Harry Redknapp became the manager of Tottenham Hotspurs the team was in the doldrums and they'd only taken 2 points all season. Over the next 5 weeks, however, they won 4 matches, drew once and scored 18 goals. How did this happen? Harry had gone in and told them, "Alright lads, listen to me, you can do this because you're all good lads ..." The players believed him and went out onto the pitch and played completely differently. He had managed to restore the joy into their game.

Being expressive in worship
True joy cannot help but be spilt over into our worship:

> *"And all the people went up after him; and the people played the flutes and rejoiced with great joy, so that the*

earth seemed to split with their sound."
(1 Kings 1:40 NKJV)

At the time this was written people didn't have a personal Spirit-filled relationship with God like we have today, but still they were motivated to manifest great joy. Why is it that we, who are meant to be filled with the Holy Spirit, sit on our backsides with our arms glued to our sides?! Our joy must be seen and heard! It grieves me when I go to places all round the country and there's no joy. When we consider the goodness of God and all that He's done for us, surely it must release joy in us and through us.

Being grateful for God's goodness

> *"You have put gladness in my heart, more than in the season that their grain and wine increased."*
> (Psalm 4:7 NKJV)

The psalmist here is choosing to remember the gladness God has given him and compares it to the riches of the earth. Think of the best thing that ever happened to you in your life, the most wonderful time. It could be your marriage, the birth of your first child, your first job, getting a pay rise or going on an incredible trip. Think of the best time you've ever had and remember that the joy God gives you exceeds that.

Being aware of your joy levels

David, having sinned, lost his inner joy. He was bereft of peace. Grace had been violated. So what was his heart's cry to the Lord?

> *"Restore to me the joy of Your salvation, and uphold me by Your generous Spirit."* (Psalm 51:12 NKJV)

Perhaps you know this feeling right now. Maybe if you are honest, you are sitting there reading this feeling bored and miserable, critical of God and His people and there's no joy in your life. The first thing to leave us in times of compromise or challenge is our joy. We try to find an excuse to blame somebody else, but actually we have just lost our joy.

Note that what David asked for was not joy by itself, but the joy of *salvation*. David knew that his salvation was precious. He did not take it for granted. Habakkuk too revealed his understanding of the same principle:

> *"Yet I will rejoice in the* Lord, *I will joy in the God of my salvation."*
>
> (Habakkuk 3:18 NKJV)

So, with all that God has done for us, it is our salvation that brings the greatest joy. Mother Teresa said, "Joy is a net of love by which you can catch a net of souls."

When was the last time you thanked God for your eternal destiny?

Being filled with the fruit of the Spirit
Galatians 5:22 speaks of the characteristics that live in every true believer, the character of Christ and His DNA. If we are going to be joyful people we need to manifest the fruits of the Spirit, especially love, joy and peace. Love, of course, is who God is. Through the knowledge of His love we are motivated and provoked to be joyful.

Being mature
I love the church I am a part of, but (like most church families) we have got a long way to go before we're a truly joyful church. We are not alone. I travel to churches all

round the country and see 50-year olds who have not learnt the maturing principle of Christ-like joy.

People say things like, "I want to be fed, I want to be taught, nobody loves me or visits me, nobody phones me or cares ..."

The boss doesn't phone us when we don't go into work. In fact, if he phones us first, it probably means we're fired! Yet people in the church often complain, "I'm not going there again. It's been five weeks and nobody's phoned me ..." I think if you haven't got the courage to phone the church and say you've got a problem, then why should your pastor phone you? You never phone him to see if he's got a problem and he probably doesn't expect you to! The bottom line is: our being joyful is not the responsibility of someone else. It is a lifestyle choice that we are in control of.

Being convinced that joy is strength

Sometimes we go through difficult and trying things. Today, I had to go into an intensive care unit to visit a young man fighting for his life. I'm having to think about what I can say to his young bride. Do you think I relish doing that today? No.

Well, what made me do it? The joy of the Lord. The joy of the Lord is my strength! What allows me to come to church and pray for the sick every week, seeing some healed and some not make it? I'll tell you: knowing that the joy of the Lord is my strength. I have all the pressures of the day, and the pressures of the church, and am aware that the economy is suffering and we've got 35 staff to look after.

Then we have meetings where everyone disagrees with one another and yet everybody's "heard from God"! What helps me to carry on? The joy of the Lord! Then I go home and my wife's in acute pain and the Lord has not healed her yet. What helps me keep praying for her? The joy of the Lord!

The book of Nehemiah starts with tears as he weeps over the broken walls of Jerusalem and ends with such joy that even outside Jerusalem other people noticed, and were affected by their rejoicing:

> *"Also that day they offered great sacrifices, and rejoiced, for God had made them rejoice with great joy; the women and the children also rejoiced, so that the joy of Jerusalem was heard afar off."*
> (Nehemiah 12:43 NKJV)

It was all due to the joy of the Lord being their strength.

Being joyful in all circumstances

Joy is the God-given antidote to the rigours of sorrow. Not all tears are destructive. Jesus wept over the death of Lazarus and many have wept over Jerusalem. Yet in this release is a reality of hope.

> *"Those who sow in tears will reap with songs of joy.*
> *He who goes out weeping, carrying seed to sow,*
> *will return with songs of joy, carrying sheaves with him."*
> (Psalm 126:5-6 NIV)

The sorrow of compassion brings a definite return of joy.
Jude 1:24 says,
"Now to Him who is able to keep you from stumbling,
And to present you faultless Before the presence of His glory with exceeding joy,"
(Jude 1:24 NKJV)

Peter teaches this:

> "Though now you do not see Him, yet believing, you rejoice with joy inexpressible and full of glory, receiving the end of your faith—the salvation of your souls. Of this salvation the prophets have inquired and searched carefully, who prophesied of the grace that would come to you."
>
> (1 Peter 1:8-10 NKJV)

You and I are going to go through pain and we might go through sacrifice, but the Bible says that it is possible to be:

> "....joyful in hope, patient in affliction, faithful in prayer."
>
> (Romans 12:12 NIV)

If you're going through a sickness at the moment can you see what's behind it and be joyful in hope? If you are in pain at the moment, can you be patient in affliction?

2 Timothy gives us such hope:

> "I know whom I have believed and am persuaded that He is able to keep what I have committed to Him until that Day."
>
> (2 Timothy 1:12 NKJV)

What day is he speaking of? The day when you and I die.

We can be joyful because, no matter what anyone does to us in this life, we have somewhere amazing to go in eternity and someone amazing to share that eternity with. Our big concern, every one of us, is not where we're going but how we're going to get there. But, if we've got the joy of the Lord it will even take us through that.

Being joyful in the right things
Recently my wife and I had a look around a bike shop. I used to cycle 200 miles a week, but when I had a heart attack the doctor told me I wasn't allowed to cycle any more, knowing full well that I could never go at it gently! He actually "banned" me from ever owning a bike again. I was 42 years old then and now I'm 65.

Looking around that shop I felt the temptation to buy a bike! I looked at the kinds of bike I used to ride, with tiny saddles, and then a few more sedate models, and I would have loved to try one out, but I walked away.

Cycling was once my joy. But it's not now. *He* is my joy.

Football was once my joy. But it's not now. *He* is my joy.

Can you say the same? There's nothing wrong with football, nothing wrong with cycling, nothing wrong with any sport, nothing wrong with your house or your car or your career, but what's your joy found in? There's nothing wrong with your girlfriend or boyfriend, husband or wife, but you can't find your eternal joy in them. My wife is not my joy factor. When I first met her she was my "wow factor" but she was not my joy factor. If my wife ever becomes my joy factor then I'm in trouble. It's the joy of the Lord that's my strength! After a date with Molly, I used to walk all the way home in the winter after missing the bus, just so I could spend a few more precious minutes with her, all because of the love I had for her. But I tell you this: it's the joy of the Lord that causes me to run and not grow weary, to walk and not grow faint.

Thinking it through:

"One joy shatters a hundred griefs."
(Chinese Proverb)

If you're a Christian I want you to ask yourself this question: If I do not have, by nature, joy welling up in me all the time, what am I going to do about it? Maybe you need to ask God to sort out the priorities in your life so that in His presence there is fullness of joy for you?

◊ What do you feel concerned and anxious about?
◊ How can you come to God and be joyful in these circumstances?
◊ What can you do to become more joyful?

Perhaps you might like to use this prayer:

"Father, please forgive me because I've allowed things to rob me of my joy. But no more! The joy of the Lord will be my strength. I shall run and not grow weary; I shall walk and not grow faint. I'll rise on wings of eagles because the joy will be the lift, will be the smile upon my face and the beat within my heart.

Forgive me, Lord, for allowing common happiness to invade me and masquerade as Your joy. Help me know again the joy that comes from Your salvation and grant that I may be joyful in hope, patient in affliction and faithful in prayer. Amen."

CHAPTER 8
The Ultimate Expression of Giving and Receiving

"The value of a man resides in what he gives and not in what he is capable of receiving."

—*Albert Einstein*

Why should we give?

We serve a God who loves to give to us. James 1:17 says that,

> *"Every good and perfect gift comes down from the Father."*   CEV

1 Chronicles 29:12 and Deuteronomy 8:18 teach us that both wealth and honour come from God. It is God who gives us all we need. He also gives us the desire and ability to pass on His blessings to others. Jesus is quoted by Luke as saying,

> *"It is more blessed to give than to receive."*
>   (Acts 20:35 NIV)

and by Matthew as teaching,

> *"Freely you have received, freely give."*
> (Matthew 10:8 NIV)

The word "give" means to present something voluntarily without expecting compensation. It is giving with no expectation of being repaid. Some people believe that giving works on some kind of formula: if I give, then God will give back to me. But giving is not meant to be prescriptive in this way. We are not meant to give from a pot that runs dry, or a heart that expects return, but from the overflowing grace and abundance that we have been given through Christ.

Giving without condition

If we give £100 to someone we should not expect anything back. If God chooses to bless us, that is wonderful, but it is not why we give. If we are honest, most of us find this sort of giving very hard. I've heard people say, "You know, Pastor Dave, I gave somebody some money once – I knew they were in need – and you should see what they did with it! I'm never going to give them anything again."

I say, "You didn't really give it to them in the first place then."

"I did! I gave them £100! But never again!"

I say, "You never really *gave* it to them. Part of you was holding on to the money as if it was still yours!"

Once we've given money away to someone, then it's nothing to do with us any more. Whatever they spend it on is not our business. If God tells you to give a sum of money to someone, you have to do that and walk away. Of course, it's nice to know that the money we have given has blessed someone or made a real difference to their family. But that isn't *why* we should give. Giving is a matter of obedience, not charity. Jesus did not say, "Give if you feel like it, or if you have some spare money that week." He said, "Freely you have received, so give freely."

I'm not advocating that we give money away to people who we know are going to be tempted to use it unwisely. That is not kind or helpful to anyone. If a person struggles to steward their money well, we can buy them food vouchers or the actual thing they are in need of. But once we have given something, it is no longer ours. If you get upset with what they do or don't do with it, then you've not let go of it; you've given it under a condition. There are times when God tells us to give something to someone for a specific purpose – maybe for a holiday, a private operation, or something they need. Giving can have a condition, *but the condition cannot be to please you.* It should always be something you believe God has laid on your heart.

The heart of giving

The whole Christian message is one of giving, not to justify one's actions or to earn forgiveness. The act of giving is, for a Christian, a reaction to the amazing power and love of God in Jesus. It's a response to the greatest Giver in world history!

So I don't give in the hope that God is looking. That was Cain's mistake who gave from the wrong motive (see Genesis 4). I give because it is my natural heartfelt response to the goodness of God.

The prophet Isaiah gave us in-depth revelation on the giving nature of God and the attitude that Jesus would manifest described in the actions of the cross. These words are about Jesus 700 years before He was even born:

> *"I gave My back to those who struck Me,*
> *And My cheeks to those who plucked out the beard;*
> *I did not hide My face from shame and spitting.*
> *For the Lord G*OD *will help Me;*
> *Therefore I will not be disgraced;*
> *Therefore I have set My face like a flint,*
> *And I know that I will not be ashamed."*
>
> (Isaiah 50:6-7 NKJV)

So before Jesus came to earth as a man, God's plan was that He would have His back ripped open and His beard pulled out. And yet He still chose to give His Son in this way. Now that's what I call giving!

Most of us know the passage of John 3:16-17 so well that we forget what it actually *means*:

> *"For God so loved the world that He gave His only begotten Son, that whoever believes in Him should not perish but have everlasting life. For God did not send His Son into the world to condemn the world, but that the world through Him might be saved."*   NKJV

We forget that God's deep love for us meant that He was led to give the most precious offering He had for us – His Son.

Giving for better, for worse

Note this: God's giving came from His heart of extreme love for us. *"For God **so** loved..."* Unless there is love, giving will always be conditional and measured. We don't sacrifice things for people we don't care for. Our pockets are never touched unless our heart is first. Jesus went to the cross because He loved you and me so much that He was prepared to endure the agony. As the writer to the Hebrews says in chapter 12:2:

> *"Let us fix our eyes on Jesus, the author and perfecter of our faith, who for the joy set before him endured the cross."* NIV

Incredibly, "the joy set before him" spoken of in this verse was the relationship with you and me. He loved us more than He feared the grave. While we were still sinners Christ gave Himself for us (see Romans 5:8). When you can love someone or something more than the sacrifice involved, you will give and give even if it hurts. What causes somebody with a disabled child, who has to be nursed day and night, to work tirelessly to give that child all he or she needs? It is "giving love". What causes a woman to nurse her dying husband for years? Does she, when she's singled out, feel embarrassed because she says "wouldn't any wife do the same?" She does it because of her deep love and commitment to him.

When you love somebody you'll do anything for them. The vows you make on your wedding day, ask you to promise that you will love someone even in sickness, poverty and problems. Love takes you through those times; love keeps you strong in those times. Even though you may be challenged in those times, true selfless love will carry you through because the love is greater than the sacrifice. We will give to people we love, even when it is costly.

God's giving nature

People sometimes say to me, "Pastor Dave, why is it that Christians often don't get healed and die but non-Christians get healed and just walk away from church and never come back? Why does that happen?" My answer is always about the giving nature of God.

Non-Christians only have this life and when they die they go to an eternity without God, what the Bible calls hell. I believe that because God is a loving God, slow to anger and abounding in love (Psalm 103:8), He delights in giving people the chance to find Him. If it comes to whether a non-Christian or a Christian should die, who is going to be better off in eternity?

Would it be unreasonable if God said, "Only pray for non-Christians because I want to keep them alive as long as possible to allow them the chance to get born again"? Would it be unreasonable to put a notice up on the screens in church that said, "Only come for prayer if you're not a Christian because the rest of us know where we're going"?

You wouldn't blame God if He said that, but in His grace He heals Christian and non-Christian alike. We get lots of Sikhs and Hindus in our healing meetings at church, and also Buddhists and Muslims. Many of them go home healed! God is giving them the opportunity to witness His giving nature for themselves.

He wants us to give, in the same way He does.

In Matthew 5:42 it says,

"Give to him who asks you."

and in Matthew 6:2 (NIV) it says,

"....give to the needy."

Again, in Matthew 19:21 (NIV) we read,

"... sell your possessions and give to the poor."

Jesus: the ultimate gift

It's great when God heals us, but Jesus died on a cross not simply to heal us but to save us from our sins. He died to save us from an eternity of separation from God. He gave His life as a ransom for many.

In 1 Timothy 2:5-6 it says this:

"For there is one God and one Mediator between God and men, the Man Christ Jesus, who gave Himself a ransom for all, to be testified in due time ..."

God says, "I'll buy back anybody's shabby life." Two years ago we were at the brink of the biggest bank collapse in history. The Bank of England actually admitted that they were within hours of total meltdown. Never before in British history had this happened where every single bank was on the verge of going under.

The Bank of England, the Government and the FSA all came together and didn't know what to do. It was worse than the 1930s' depression. They didn't believe it could happen. It suddenly started to snowball and none of them knew what to do.

Our lives are like that without God; utterly barren and bankrupt. But God still chooses to buy us back! The gift of God, of His son, has brought reconciliation and restored relationship with Him. We're not only redeemed and restored, we're reconciled.

"For unto us a Child is born, unto us a Son is given."
(Isaiah 9:6 NKJV)

Why did He say that the son was *given*? It's because the first born always has a right to his father's inheritance. When

Jesus was given to the world, all the resources of heaven came with Him. What a gift to us that is!

Because of this amazing truth we become part of God's family:

"God's Spirit doesn't make us slaves who are afraid of him. Instead, we become his children and call him our Father. God's Spirit makes us sure that we are his children. His Spirit lets us know that together with Christ we will be given what God has promised. We will also share in the glory of Christ, because we have suffered with him. I am sure that what we are suffering now cannot compare with the glory that will be shown to us. In fact, all creation is eagerly waiting for God to show who his children are."

(Romans 8:15-19 CEV)

This passage teaches us that we are given the gift of adoption. We become God's children so we can call Him "Abba Father". Now we are fathered, loved, encouraged and given wisdom and counsel and protection. And all this because He's such a giving God!

He gave Abraham the covenant of wisdom; He gave Moses the Ten Commandments; He gave to us the Body and Blood of His Son; He gave the children of Israel food in the wilderness, fire by night and a cloud by day; He gave the five thousand food; He gave the widow her son back; He gave the blind their sight; He gave the gift of the Holy Spirit; He gave a promise that He would return to His Church; He promised us the resurrection from the grave. I could go on!

Just look at all He has given to us! How does it make you want to respond?

Give as you have been given to

We now have the ability to give. I am not just talking about giving financially, but giving of ourselves in worship, giving our time, our energy and our talents. There are 910 scriptures on giving in the Bible. Numerous times it says:

> *"Give thanks to the LORD."*
> (e.g. Psalm 7:17 NIV)

We are taught that,

> *"Each man should give what he has decided in his heart to give, not reluctantly or under compulsion, for God loves a cheerful giver."*
> (2 Corinthians 9:7 NIV)

But we often don't look or act as if we are at all cheerful about all He has done for us! I sometimes think that if our children showed as much gratitude as we do to God, we'd wonder what we'd done to them! You often hear more noise in a cinema than you do in a church! Some people maintain that their faith is something very personal and very private, but the Bible suggests the opposite. If the devil can keep your mouth shut and the smile off your face and the attitude of gratitude out of your heart, he's stopped the greatest weapon you've got. We've got to give God thanks; we've got to give Him praise. It changes whole situations when we release words of affirmation about who God is. Some of us don't get the breakthrough we crave or keep our healing because we don't continually live in thankfulness to God.

The Bible says,
> *"And my mouth **shall** show forth Your praise."*
> (Psalm 51:15 NKJV)

The word "praise" means to make bodily gesture. "Worship" means to bow and kiss. So if you are a worshipper or a praiser, I will be able to see it in how you act in bodily manifestation. Quietness and stillness are spoken of in the Bible as something that God gives, in between praise and worship. It's a small, reflective interval; it isn't the main performance.

We need to remember that we aren't going to get a quiet time in heaven. How can you not praise God when you see Him in all His glory? How can you keep from singing? How can you stop praising? How can you not worship Him? Myriads of angels and all the company of heaven will be joining in with the adoration of God. Its going to be amazing!

Giving to God

What then can you give God? You can give Him your heart; you can give Him your praise; you can give Him your worship; you can give Him the desires of your heart; you can give Him your unresolved issues. You can give Him so much! My prayer is that, in this year coming, you and I don't allow the spirit of religion to rob us of what we can receive or give.

We need to remember that, when we give God something in the right spirit, He honours that:

> *"Give away your life; you'll find life given back, but not merely given back—given back with bonus and blessing. Giving, not getting, is the way. Generosity begets generosity."*
>
> (Luke 6:38 The Message)

Another version of this verse describes how God gives to us:

> *"Your gift will return to you in full—pressed down, shaken together to make room for more, running over, and poured into your lap."*
>
> (NLT)

People sometimes say to me that I work too hard for God. But when I look back over my life, I remember that there are at least 7 times I should have died. God has kept me alive. He has given me life and life to the full! I couldn't read or write until I got saved! He has given me access to the truth of His Word so that I can preach and teach others. That's my generous God!

But with great respect, I'm no special man. I take responsibilities on my shoulders and of course I get tired, but I see it as normal to want to please Him; it's normal to want to worship Him; it's normal to want to serve Him; it's normal to want to give for Him; it's normal to want to love people; it's normal to have compassion; it's normal to show mercy; it's normal to forgive; it's normal to pray for the sick. I am just seeking to do what it says in the Word.

I'm sure I could give Him more, but I constantly try to live remembering all He has done for me.

> *"Forget not all His benefits."*
>
> (Psalm 103:2 NKJV)

What about you? How do you live? Are you giving your all for the One who gave His all for you?

Thinking it through:

Winston Churchill said this: "We make a living by what we get, but we make a life by what we give."

Take some time out to ask, "Lord, how much have you given me?" Maybe you could even write down all of your blessings.

Then you could ask, "Lord, do I grumble when I give to You? By your Spirit show me whether I have a giving nature, in my worship and praise, finances and time, and in my friendships. Am I a giving person?" If the answer is no, what a great present you can receive today: His forgiveness!

◊   In what areas do you think you are a giving person?
◊   Where could you be more generous?

Maybe you could say the words of this prayer as you dwell on these thoughts:

"Father God, I want to thank You that my faith comes from a giving God. I want to be a giving person both in my body and in my spirit, with my mind and with my soul. I want to be passionate for Your Word and Your Name. I want to be able to give to You and to others in every area of my life. I want to be a witness to everyone I know and love.

I pray now that my love for you will always be greater than my sacrifice. Amen."

CHAPTER

9 *Mercy*

"To you, O Lord, belongs mercy."
(Psalm 62:12 NKJV)

Defining mercy

The Bible tells us that God's mercy endures forever and His mercy is mentioned frequently throughout Scripture. But what exactly is mercy?

Mercy can be defined as the act of showing compassion or clemency to those who are under our power. Mercy occurs when one who has the ability to punish another, willingly (not begrudgingly) releases the perpetrator of the offence. Some biblical commentators have summed this up by saying, "Mercy is compassion to the miserable" because, by default, the person who is in need of mercy is usually in desperate circumstances.

This is the original idea behind being "at someone's mercy". Mercy does not release a person from the crime they have committed, but can excuse or minimise the penalty for that crime. We can decide to let someone off when they have committed an offence against us – if we are in a position to do so.

Mercy is born out of a heart of compassion. It is having compassion on someone who has been caught red-handed and deciding to show them a kindly benevolence. The clearest analogy is that of a High Court Judge whose job is to pass sentence on an offender who has been found guilty of a crime. Depending on the circumstances of the case, the judge can act with severe retribution or he can mitigate the punishment that is meted out. He even has the power to pardon the offender, if he considers it appropriate to do so. The judge is the only person who has the authority to dictate the sentence. He can choose to be merciful or he can choose to bring the full weight of his powers to bear.

I act as chairman for the board of a local council organisation and one of my responsibilities is to handle disciplinary issues. Recently, I had to listen to the details of a particular case and decide on an appropriate level of punishment for an offence that had been committed. After hearing the facts of the case, I had to give a judgement and spell out the punishment that would follow. I commented on the mitigating circumstances, surrounding the incident and then told the person what their punishment was. Because of the circumstances, I showed mercy to the person. They still had to be punished, but I made it clear that they were not receiving as severe a punishment as they could have received.

In the UK, historically the Monarch always held the power to pardon those who had been given the death sentence. Later, before the UK abolished capital punishment, people could also appeal to the Home Secretary who had the power to commute a sentence to life imprisonment. Similarly, in the US, the Governor of a state can be appealed to for clemency. But if he denies the appeal, then the person will end up on death row and eventually be executed.

The legal system, the concept of administering justice, punishment being meted out to fit a particular crime, and the idea of that punishment being minimised or pardoned – all of these are earthly pictures that help us to understand the righteous judgement of God and how amazing is His divine mercy towards us.

The qualities of mercy

Coming under judgement leads us to feel condemned, fearful, rejected and worthless. But being shown mercy causes us to rejoice because we know we are not getting what we thoroughly deserve. The reason we grow in Christ is that we trust that God will be merciful to us as we fumble through life; making mistakes, falling over and getting back up again. Psalm 13:5 says,

"I have trusted in Your mercy; and my heart shall rejoice in Your salvation."   NKJV

Mercy is a quality that tells us something important about the character of God. It reveals the very essence of who He is. Mercy is one of a cluster of similar attributes of God that work closely together. Alongside His mercy we see God's *grace* and His *compassion.* They are like three distinct yet complimentary stones that sit together to form a perfect diamond ring.

Compassion, is God reaching down to touch with kindness those who do not deserve it, like Jesus washing His disciples' feet – especially the feet of the man who Jesus knew was going to betray Him. Compassion can also be defined as serving those who socially, economically, academically, or for any other reason, are disadvantaged compared to us.

Grace shows God to be someone who bestows gifts upon people who have never, ever deserved it. His grace is an act of benevolence towards us.

Compassion and grace compliment mercy perfectly. The only difference is, whilst grace and compassion are gifts to the undeserving, mercy is a gift to those who *are* deserving – deserving of punishment.

Like the High Court Judge, divine mercy does not act as if no offence was committed. That is not mercy. God does not wink at sin and say, "Don't worry about that, let's brush it under the carpet." The penalty for sin must always be paid by someone. The ultimate act of God's mercy was providing a sacrifice for our sins. We could not pay for our own sins – the price was way beyond our means – so God made His Son, Jesus, who did not know sin, to become sin for us and pay the price. God's greatest act of mercy towards us is that we deserve to be in hell, but we are spared from it because of Jesus' sacrifice. Receiving this gift of mercy is dependent upon us repenting of our sins and confessing Jesus as our Saviour.

The most amazing quality of God's mercy is that it is an act of kindness and favour from the heart of a loving Father. The roots of the word itself carry the idea of receiving a "heavenly reward" or "gift". This tells us that mercy is, first and foremost, a divine quality derived from the nature of God. It has no origin in mankind. "Mercy" is a God-word – He invented it. Our reaction to this should be, "Wow!" When a man in the dock, who is expecting a severe custodial sentence is released, what else can he say other than, "What a relief! Thank you so much!"?

Are we as thankful for God's mercy towards us as we should be? Especially if we pause for a moment and recall all the sins we have committed that God could punish us for, but chooses not to? People often mistake God's mercy for Him being blasé about sin. When we don't get the punishment we deserve, we can mistakenly think that God is *allowing* the sin as if it doesn't matter or He condones our actions in some way. It sounds foolish, but some people do think this way. Yet, *every* sin will ultimately have to be accounted for one day. God can't ignore our sin – it cost His Son His life.

The Mercy Seat

In Exodus 25:17-22 we see a graphic depiction of this attribute of God, in the ancient Mercy Seat that was the centrepiece of the tabernacle. It was central to the need of dealing with sin under the Old Covenant. Mercy was such an important concept to God that He made this visual representation of it, so that His people could see and understand.

The Mercy Seat was part of the Ark of the Covenant which was about 3 metres long and made of wood (which speaks of humanity) overlaid with gold (which speaks of divinity). In one sense then, the Ark was symbolic of Jesus, the Saviour to come, who was both fully man and fully God. On top of the Ark was a seat. No person could sit on this seat or even touch the Ark without dying instantly – the seat was symbolic of the fact that God comes to sit among His people, to rule and reign.

But this seat was, in reality, a seat of judgement that, if God had not designated it otherwise by giving it a certain name, would have condemned everyone to death. God allowed this seat to be used to invoke His mercy. Once a year, the High Priest, having cleansed himself and dressed in clean clothes, applied the blood of an innocent lamb to various points of his body and would then walk into the Holy of Holies where the Ark was situated.

On the Ark were two cherubim, one at each end with their wings covering the Mercy Seat. The priest would take the blood of the slaughtered lamb, dip a bunch of hyssop into it, and sprinkle the blood on the Mercy Seat. Then, when God looked upon the seat and saw the blood of the lamb, He would see mercy rather than judgement. The innocent blood evoked His mercy. It was the same principle that applied to the Children of Israel on the eve of their escape from Egypt: "When I see the blood, I will pass over you…" God's people escaped the terror of the angel of death because of the blood, and they received God's mercy rather than His wrath.

God is not angry!

This picture shows us that God would rather show mercy than mete out judgement if He can. God is a loving God, not one who is just waiting for an opportunity to squash us. The Christian faith is unique in the world because we do not come to God to appease Him because He is angry. Nearly all the other world religions have an angry god at their heart and all the actions of those religions are geared towards preventing and appeasing that anger.

Sadly, I know some Christians who believe that God is angry all the time too. They live in fear of Him, but it is not a healthy fear. They think that God is out to get them and is only concerned with stopping them from enjoying themselves. Or they think that God is waiting for them to step out of line so that He can slap them down. I cannot find any such concept of Christianity anywhere in the Bible. It's called legalism. God is full of joy and delights in showing mercy. Jesus was full of fun. He said things that, if we understood His remarks in the context of the Jewish culture of His day, were outlandish and hilarious. Two thousand years later we miss the humour of His words, but that doesn't alter the fact that Jesus was a lot of fun and a wonderful person to be around.

Real Christianity is not constantly trying to appease God and say sorry all the time. Have you ever met someone who says sorry all the time and who spends most of their time being apologetic? It's very frustrating and you just want them to get over the issue and be themselves. I can't help thinking that if people like that spend their whole time being apologetic towards others, what must they be like with God? God doesn't want us to come crawling to Him, telling Him all the time how wretched we are. Those who have put their trust in Jesus can come to Him with confidence and have the assurance of His acceptance and mercy.

The conditional nature of God's mercy

In James 2:12-13 we read a profoundly shocking statement. James writes,

> *"Speak and act as those who are going to be judged by the law that gives freedom, because judgment without mercy will be shown to anyone who has not been merciful. Mercy triumphs over judgment!"* NIV

God has been magnanimous is showing mercy towards us when He could rightfully wipe us out. But if we then refuse to show mercy to others in return, what then? What happens is that we stem the flow of God's mercy to us. James is saying that if we do not practise mercy ourselves, if we don't have compassion on those who wrong us, neither will God have mercy on us – and if we are not under God's mercy, we are certainly under His judgement.

This simple equation explains why so many people live unhappy lives. People wrong us and offend us, often – it is a fact of life – but we must show them mercy and forgive them. If we don't, if we harbour feelings of bitterness and unforgiveness, then we are judging those people and by doing so, bringing ourselves under judgement. Whenever we meet a person who is harshly critical, it is usually because they have unforgiveness in their life, which in turn robs them of mercy and compassion as they live under the judgement of God. This is why it is so important to forgive.

The unmerciful servant

Jesus taught His followers a salutary lesson on this in the parable of the unmerciful servant. One modern Bible version helps put this story into context by putting the amounts of money involved into today's currency.

The story goes, a man is arrested for owing a large amount of money to a ruler – about £5,000. The law of the land stipulates that any person unwilling or unable to repay a loan is put into prison, so the man appears before the ruler, cannot pay his debt and is duly imprisoned.

These are dire circumstances indeed. Since the man is in prison he can't work, and if he can't work then he can't repay his debt, so basically he will remain in prison forever! But, he is in a situation of his own making. He borrowed the money and he didn't pay it back. The ruler has every right to insist on him being jailed because that is the law.

The ruler, however, seeing the man's desperate situation, decides to have mercy on him. He has spent a short time languishing in prison, no doubt pondering his own and his family's fate, when he is brought before the ruler again. The ruler says, "You're here because you deserve to be here. This is your punishment. But, I am going to show you mercy and release you. I forgive your debt." Notice that the ruler does not say, "Now, get out to work and start repaying this debt!" He writes the debt off altogether and releases the man without penalty.

Now the man who has been set free and forgiven his debt, walks out of the prison. He must have been overjoyed to have his punishment drastically reduced, but even more so to have his debt removed altogether. Then he bumps into a fellow servant who owes *him* some money. This man owes him 90p – under £1 – but he can't pay it. On hearing this, one would think that the first man would be merciful and let him off, but no, he beats him up a bit and then has *him* thrown into prison!

Let's look at this incident a bit more closely before we jump to any conclusions. 90p doesn't sound a lot compared to £5,000, but the man still owed the money and had not repaid it, so he had broken the law too. He was in the same position as the first servant. Have you ever been in a public car park and needed to pay £1 to get out through the barrier – but you only have 90p? For the sake of 10p you can't pay and you're not going anywhere! This story is not about "amounts" at all. The first man had broken the law and the second man had broken the law too. They had both sinned. Jesus was not saying that the second man deserved to be let off because his was only a little sin. There are no levels of sin! The first servant was right to take the second man to the judge because he did owe him money which he had not repaid.

Some time later, however, the ruler in the story discovers that the servant has had this man imprisoned for owing him money. The amount of money is irrelevant – it is the fact that the servant who was shown mercy was not practising mercy himself that enraged the ruler. The ruler then has the unmerciful servant dragged back in to see him and says, "I am revoking my mercy off your life, because you are not living in the goodness of it. Now you will go to prison and rot in hell!"

What this teaches us is: mercy is only effective as long as we abide in it. We have to "live" in mercy in order to receive it. The same is true of forgiveness, grace and love. We cannot trample all over these God-given gifts and still expect to receive them from Him in abundance. The Bible says,

> "Blessed are the merciful for they shall be shown mercy."
>
> (Mathew 5:7 NIV)

The day we stop showing mercy to others is the day we stop receiving it ourselves. Much of what we receive from God is conditional, but we don't often hear that preached today. Many preach a message of, "Put up your hand and respond to God and you're in the club. Don't forget to become a member of the church's Facebook group and you're home and dry!" I think not! What God has done for us, we are bound to do for others.

God's great mercy

The good news is that mercy triumphs over judgement, because that is God's heart. In Exodus 34:5-8 we read God's description of Himself to Moses:

> "Yahweh! The LORD!
> The God of compassion and mercy!
> I am slow to anger
> and filled with unfailing love and faithfulness.
> I lavish unfailing love to a thousand generations.
> I forgive iniquity, rebellion, and sin.
> But I do not excuse the guilty.
> I lay the sins of the parents upon their children and grandchildren;

*the entire family is affected—
even children in the third and fourth generations."*

NLT

God's mercy extends to thousands of generations, but He mitigates His judgement, only allowing it to extend as far as four generations at the most. God must judge where people will not receive His mercy, but His heart is to extend His mercy to a thousand generations. 1 Chronicles 16:34 says,

"Oh, give thanks to the LORD for He is good! For His mercy endures forever."

NKJV

Practise mercy

Christianity is lived out, not by keeping a set of rules, but by living a set of values. If we remember to be merciful then we will live in God's mercy ourselves. In Matthew 9:13 Jesus said,

"Go and learn what this means: 'I desire mercy and not sacrifice.' For I did not come to call the righteous, but sinners, to repentance."

NKJV

Note what Jesus said. We need to go and *learn*. Mercy is not a natural gift, it must be learned and we learn it by practising it. Mercy requires a willingness on our part to demonstrate this attribute of God to others.

In Matthew 23:23 Jesus pointed out that the Pharisees prayed and paid their tithes, yet they neglected what He said were the weightier matters of the law: justice, mercy and faith. The fact is, you can pay your tithe, give to the church building fund, and be a leader in your church, but if you lack mercy then God says you've got everything back to front!

Christianity is not everything we have received from God – it is everything we have received from Him that we are prepared to do for others. If God has forgiven you, then you need to be a forgiving person. If God has blessed you, you need to bless others. If God has given to you, you need to be a person who gives. Sin deserves judgement, but mercy can minimise that judgement. If someone sins against you, show them mercy.

It was Abraham Lincoln who said, "I've always found that mercy bears richer fruits than strict justice." And John Bunyan, the author of *Pilgrim's Progress*, said, "Sin is the rape of His mercy." God has been so incredibly merciful not to send us to hell that we should never abuse or take that fact for granted. The Bible says, "Mercy shall follow me all the days of my life."

Thank God for the manifestation of His kindness.

Thinking it through:

Why not write down how God and other people have not judged you as you deserved but have shown you mercy.

◊ Now consider the times that you have done the same. Or situations that you still now need to address.

◊ Before you read the next chapter you may have to make that phone call, write that letter or visit that friend or relative and put into practise that which you have just read.

CHAPTER 10
Tangible Peace

> *"For to us a child is born, to us a son is given, and the government will be on his shoulders. And he will be called Wonderful Counsellor, Mighty God, Everlasting Father, Prince of Peace."*
>
> (Isaiah 9:6 NIV)

> *"First keep the peace within yourself then you can also bring peace to others."*
>
> —Thomas à Kempis

In this chapter, I am going to unpack one of the most basic and yet profound aspects of Christian truth. Jesus is the giver of deep, tangible, eternal and wonderful peace and I believe that to live in this kind of peace is an attainable reality for us.

When we grasp this truth for ourselves, in all its depth and yet its simplicity, we will experience what it means to know a peace that defies human reasoning. Philippians 4:7 says:

> *"And the peace of God, which transcends all understanding, will guard your hearts and your minds in Christ Jesus."*

We are not talking about a peace that leaves us the minute life gets hard, or a peace that Jesus loans to us just for the valleys of life, but a lasting, undergirding peace, that anchors our very souls and guards our hearts.

I pray that as you read this, whatever the circumstances of your life today, you would sense the Prince of Peace beginning to reign afresh in your heart.

༺ ༻

I have some friends in the church I pastor who were married for 42 years. Mavis and Lenny knew each other closely and beautifully; they had a lovely relationship. Mavis knew Lenny in a way that no one else knew him and vice versa. When he died recently, she was in church that very evening, praising and giving thanks to God. Such is the level of her peace in her life.

Stop and take a personal inventory for a moment. How are your peace levels right now? What are the trials you are going through that are threatening to rob you of your peace?

Let me tell you something. When we have true intimacy with the Father and true relationship with the Son and the Holy Spirit, whatever we go through, we can still hold on to a real spiritual, tangible peace. Do you need to know the truth of that today?

A heart at peace

In life people know us for different things, don't they? Maybe we are thought of as the serious one at work, or the one who is always generous. Perhaps we are known in our family as a peacemaker (or a trouble-maker!). Any time our name is mentioned to another person, it conjures up an image in their mind of our character.

So what are you known for? Are you known as a "person of peace", or are you better known as a "person in pieces"? We all have many roles in life. You might be someone's mother or father, someone's boss, someone's brother or sister, or someone's friend.

You are *one* person, but you are known to each person who knows you, uniquely. What can these people see of the Prince of Peace in your character and in your spirit? If everyone who knows you got together to compare notes about you, would they all say the same things? It's challenging to consider, isn't it?

I used to be involved in the world of financial management in football. If a footballer comes into the church I pastor now (as they sometimes do), will they see the same man they knew in the dressing room or at a board meeting? I pray they do. I want to be a man of consistent character; a man who lives a life of peace.

When our hearts are able to be at peace, all sorts of things change:

1. our attitude
2. our knowledge
3. our security
4. our prayers

Our attitude

When we know a deep peace from God, it may not change our circumstances. We may still have cancer, or live in financial difficulty. We may still struggle with the same issues. But the way we feel about those things changes. A peaceful heart is one that is "guarded". It is able to be shielded from some of the stresses and strife of life. We can rise above the situations and problems that are seeking to weigh us down; we can be transformed to think and feel differently, even if nothing on the outside changes.

Our Knowledge

In order to have deep peace, we need a deep knowledge of the *peace-giver*. How do we know if something in our life is from God or not? How do we know if a person speaking from the platform is truly relaying God's heart to us? We only know through the intimacy of knowing Him and what He is like.

A lovely lady came to me once and said she had stopped praying for her husband to be saved. She had read a book on predestination and had become convinced that her husband was going to hell. I was saddened that she had been so led off track. Because I know the person of God and I know His Word, I know that *my God* would never tell her to do such a thing or make a person believe that, and I was able to correct her.

Even if you haven't got your Bible with you to check what someone is saying, if you have knowledge of the Scriptures and knowledge of Him, you will know what is and isn't consistent with God's character. Such knowledge brings peace.

Our security

I'm good with babies. I'm not a genius, but I've learnt over the years that what a baby most needs is to feel secure and safe. So when I hold a little one, I talk and sing to him or her very gently. I hold their face close to mine so they can feel the vibration of my voice – a bit like they would have heard their mother's heart beat in the womb. The baby will often become mesmerised and still. Why? Because they feel safe and secure.

Jesus longs to share His peace with us in the same way. Often, when we pray for people at church, they become still and deeply relaxed. They sense Jesus speaking to them by His Holy Spirit and suddenly start to feel secure and safe again. This is when His peace can begin its work.

Our prayers

When we are in chaos and turmoil we don't pray well, do we? Let's face it, it's difficult to pray when we are in pain or anxious about something. When life throws something unexpected our way, it's often hard to take it to God. But when we have the deep, lasting tangible peace of Christ, even our prayers change. Perhaps we might not pray for our burdens to be lifted, but for a stronger back to bear them.

The gift of peace

When Jesus left this world 2,000 years ago to return to His Father, He left us a gift. Often Christians get this next bit wrong. They think this gift was the Holy Spirit. I want you to understand this! The Holy Spirit is *not* a gift, He is fully and completely God. Jesus didn't bequeath us the Holy Spirit as His leaving present. But He did say this in John 16:7 (NIV):

> *"I tell you the truth: It is for your good that I am going away. Unless I go away, the Counsellor will not come to you; but if I go, I will send him to you."*

In other words, Jesus is saying, "It is to your advantage that I go away, because if I go, He will come." The Godhead are not in competition with one another. They work together, but they do not rival one another. Look at what Jesus says later in verse 15 of John 16:

> *"Everything that the Father has is Mine. That is what I meant when I said that He [the Spirit] will take the things that are Mine and will reveal (declare, disclose, transmit) it to you."*
>
> (Amplified Bible)

What Jesus is underlining here is this: "Everything God has given to me will become yours." What was it that God gave to Jesus? What gift did He have that He passes on to us via the Holy Spirit? What was the last thing He gave us before He left to return to the Father in heaven? John 14:27 reveals this:

> *"Peace I leave with you; my peace I give you. I do not give to you as the world gives. Do not let your hearts be troubled and do not be afraid."*
>
> NIV

Or as the New Living Translation puts it:

> *"I am leaving you with a gift—peace of mind and heart. And the peace I give is a gift the world cannot give. So don't be troubled or afraid."*

So then, the present that Jesus gave to us was His peace. Not an ordinary, worldly kind of peace. Not a natural peace for when things are going well and there is money to last until the end of the month. Rather, His gift is an unnatural, divine, extraordinary, heavenly peace. It is nothing like the world gives. The world always gives under obligation. Any peace that the world has to offer is conditional, isn't it? The world says things like, "If you buy this house, you will feel peaceful ... If you own this type of car ... if you know these people ... if you go to this place on holiday ..." etc. But Jesus is speaking directly against that kind of "strings-attached" human understanding of wellbeing, happiness and peace. He says, "You know what? I know what you need. You need *My* peace. Not some counterfeit, fake 'here today and gone tomorrow' kind." Just read the amazing promise contained at the end of John14:27:

> *"Do not let your hearts be troubled, neither let them be afraid. Stop allowing yourselves to be agitated and disturbed; and do not permit yourselves to be fearful and intimidated and cowardly and unsettled."*
> (Amplified Bible)

We all struggle to be at peace when illness or redundancy strike. That is natural. But this verse encourages us not to allow ourselves to be "agitated or disturbed". If Jesus says it, then it must be possible!

The blessings of peace

The Greek word used in John 14:27 for peace is not the Shalom type greeting we may be familiar with. The word used here is *eirenea* which is much more about a state of tranquility. It means exemption from the rage and havoc of inner and outer war, as well as security, safety and prosperity. So, what are the blessings of this kind of peace?

1. Inner prosperity
The "prosperity" this verse speaks of is nothing to do with our financial wellbeing. It is about our very souls prospering. It is the kind of peace that comes from being assured of salvation through Christ, fearing nothing from God, being content with our earthly lot, whatever may come our way.

Jesus offers us so much. If we realised that the same Spirit who raised Him from the dead was at work in us too, we would be a much more radical people! 1 Corinthians 2:16 tells us that we have the very "mind of Christ" and that we are capable of having *His* thoughts and feelings. This means we can know and understand His peace. This is quite mind-blowing, isn't it?

What kind of people would we be if we really grasped this? We would be known not just by our love but by our ability to prosper in our soul when other people are "losing it". This kind of *prosperity peace* has an expression of completeness. If we have this kind of peace it can't get any better. Underlying it is the truth that it is "well with my soul" whatever else is going on around me. I am healed and whole in spirit, even if not in body. 3 John 1:2 puts it like this:

> *"Beloved, I pray that you may prosper in every way and [that your body] may keep well, even as [I know] your soul keeps well and prospers, I pray that you may prosper in all things and be in health."*
> (Amplified Bible)

In other words, just as your soul prospers and is successful, so your health and wellbeing mirrors that.

2. Outer stability

When we make the Word of God a priority in our lives, one of the results is that peace enters. Not just a small, transient peace but a deep, lasting "great" peace. Psalm 119:165 says:

> "**Great** *peace have they who love your law, and nothing can make them stumble.*"
>
> NIV

This knowledge and love of the Word of God has the physical effect of stabilising us. It is some promise to declare "*nothing* can make them stumble"! Peace is inner assurance of wholeness. Stable people don't fall over and they don't knock others over.

3. Restful sleep

One of the first things to leave us in times of fear, anxiety and stress is our ability to "switch off" and get restful sleep at night. It is something many of us struggle with. We all know that bad nights lead to difficult days. But the peace we are being offered in God's Word is so practical! God knows that we need deep rest. Psalm 4:8 puts that need like this:

> "*I will lie down and sleep in peace, for you alone, O LORD, make me dwell in safety.*"
>
> NIV

Maybe you are not sleeping well at the moment. Perhaps something has stolen your peace and you find that, especially at night, your mind replays the fears over and over again? Maybe you are struggling with depression or some other psychological problem?

Read this verse again:

"You alone, O LORD make me dwell in safety."

When we know that we belong to Him and that we are as safe and close to Him as the baby I mentioned earlier, we can truly rest and find peaceful sleep.

When the disciples found themselves in the midst of a storm (see Mark 4) Jesus remained fast asleep. Why was this? He was kept in perfect peace by His Father. He was secure in who He was, so He went to sleep. He knew He would die on a cross, not in a storm! He could sleep in the reality of true peace. We too can sleep "the sleep of the righteous" even when we are going through turmoil and trouble.

4. Active calm

The kind of peace Jesus offers us does not remain static. Isaiah 9:7 says,

> *"Of the increase of his government and peace there will be no end. He will reign on David's throne and over his kingdom, establishing and upholding it with justice and righteousness from that time on and forever. The zeal of the Lord Almighty will accomplish this."*
>
> NIV

In other words, the peace of Christ is active and constantly seeking to be *increased and extended* into more hearts, and more situations. His peace will not end. The result of such a peace is that it cannot help but affect our relationships with others. When we are at peace, we naturally extend that peace to those around us.

5. Changed relationships

There are countries Britain is currently "at peace" with. However, this does not necessarily mean we are in any kind of relationship with them. It simply means we are *not at war.* We can be the same with individuals we know. Just because we are at peace with someone, does not mean that we are in any kind of relationship with them. We may, in fact, be one comment away from being very much at war!

Look at what Isaiah counsels on this:

"You will guard him and keep him in perfect and constant peace whose mind [both its inclination and its character] is stayed on You, because he commits himself to You, leans on You, and hopes confidently in You."
(Isaiah 26:3 Amplified Bible)

This verse highlights for us that God will guard and keep us in a state of consistent peace if our mind, *in inclination and character is stayed on Him.* Isaiah is not talking here about merely living in *tolerance* with our surroundings and our fellow human beings. That is the kind of peace that the world offers us – a low-level, inactive acceptance. This kind of peace is built purely on the absence of anything negative. It has no substance or purpose. What we are being encouraged to dwell on here, is that we can have a peace that is perfect and constant, a peace *full* of God's own character.

The word "stayed" in the Hebrew means to "take hold of". So if our mind "takes hold of" or leans upon God's peace, the results are that we can "hope confidently in Him" whatever else comes our way.

6. Being known as peacekeepers

Did you realise that we are identified as being people of God by our peacekeeping? When I think of some families I know, and some churches too, it can be a bit of a challenge to believe it at times! But peace is an attribute of the true believer. We are called to manifest all the qualities of Sonship. Ephesians 4:3 says,

> *"Be eager and strive earnestly to guard and keep the harmony and oneness of [and produced by] the Spirit, in the binding power of peace."* (Amplified Bible)

The bond of peace mentioned here is the unity of the Spirit that we are meant to *keep*. This is not just about *making* peace, it is about guarding and keeping the unity and peace we have *already been left* by Jesus. This kind of peace balances us and allows us to bring balance and stability to others.

7. Not losing peace when trouble comes

My wife remarked recently, "Dave, I don't know what's happened to you. A lot of your aggression seems to have gone. A while ago, if someone said something that offended you, you'd be quick to sort them out. What has changed?"

It's not that I'm getting tired and old. I am just living a better way! I have learned over the years not to allow anyone to steal my peace. If someone offends or hurts me in some way, I can now release them to God and not become their judge.

When I first started out as a pastor, I wasn't secure at all. I needed a lot of affirmation. There's nothing wrong with me – we are all like that! A lot of us don't expect to get any encouragement because we have never been used to it, but we all like being praised. If someone says, "That's a nice hair-do" or "What a great church" or "What a lovely meal", we lap it up, don't we? It's natural. We all need and respond to affirmation.

But I'm more secure now than I have ever been. I don't have to prove anything. It is well with my soul. Now don't get me wrong! I am not as holy as I should be. But I am loved and secure in Him. My peace is not rocked by how others treat me, by the absence of compliments or affirmation. My peace is secure in Him. In any case, if I can lose my peace because of someone's ill humour or harsh words, was it really God's deep, tangible peace that was dwelling in me in the first place?

If you know the peace of God like this, you won't let anyone take it off you.

If we lose our peace too easily it is because it was based on our peace and not His.

If our peace cannot withstand conflict then it's not the peace of God.

8. Deep contentment

The day they ordained me as a minister was one of the happiest days of my life. It was the first time I had ever passed an exam or felt I had made a success of anything. I have turned down far greater honours since then. I honestly feel like I don't need them. Others may say, "Why didn't you take that, Dave?" but it is just not what I need to give me happiness or peace. Don't get me wrong, I like presents. Who doesn't? But if you said you wanted to buy me something and asked me what I'd like, I wouldn't be able to tell you! I'm rubbish at Christmas when my children ask me what they can get me – I'm no help at all! The reason for this is simple. I am content with what I have. The Bible says we should learn to be content in all things (see Philippians 4:11). I have learnt the deep contentment that peace brings. Things like nice cars, holidays and houses don't hold any fascination for me. Those trappings of wealth used to motivate me like you wouldn't believe, but not any more.

A minister said to me recently, "Wow! You have a big church. What do you drive? A 7-series BMW?"

I said, "No, a 5-series. It's about 7 years old and I only bought it because the dealer offered me £5K off the price."

"When are you changing it?" he asked.

"Well, it's only done 79,000 miles," I replied.

"Yes, but a man in your position ..." he began to say.

"What do you mean, a man in my position?" I asked.

"Well, you run a big church ..."

He was implying that I should drive a big, expensive car as some kind of status symbol. Big church = Big car. I'd rather spend the money on my church building fund. Why would I change my car when it's capable of doing 200,000 miles? I could drive a fiesta or a mini – it wouldn't bother me. I don't get my security from the car I drive. When you live at peace with God you can have nice things, but they are not priorities any more.

Letting peace rule

> *"Let the peace of Christ rule in your hearts, since as members of one body you were called to peace. And be thankful."*
>
> (Colossians 3:15 NIV)

If something is going to have dominion in your heart, let it be peace. Not pornography, not the love of money, or pride – let peace rule your heart. In order to do this, there first needs to be an abdication of self. The result of this selflessness is twofold. Firstly, it sanctifies us and secondly it produces righteousness.

> *"May God himself, the God of peace, sanctify you through and through. May your whole spirit, soul and body be kept blameless at the coming of our Lord Jesus Christ."*
>
> (1 Thessalonians 5:23 NIV)

> *"Peacemakers who sow in peace raise a harvest of righteousness."*
>
> (James 3:18 NIV)

Sanctification and righteousness come through peace.

Aggressive peace

We often think of peace as being mild and meek, perhaps even a bit weak! Maybe, as I mentioned earlier, we see it purely as an absence of conflict rather than a chasing after relationship or the stilling of a storm. But the peace that Jesus offers us is much more powerful than this. Read the following verse and dwell on the majesty and power you find there:

> *"He got up, rebuked the wind and said to the waves, 'Quiet! Be still.' Then the wind died down and it was completely calm."*
>
> (Mark 4:39 NIV)

This kind of peace changes natural forces with immediate effect. This kind of peace can heal bodies. This kind of peace can attack cancer and shrivel it. It can speak calm to a troubled mind. It can change a situation in seconds. What could it do for you right now, today? Whatever situation you are facing, this peace is both internal and external. It's spiritual and psychological. It's temporal and eternal. Even the most powerful fear and anxiety can be subdued by the powerful peace of Almighty God. If we walk in peace with man and in peace with God like this, we too can be a channel of His healing, blessing and peace to others.

What destroys your peace?

I know an extraordinary young man who knows an amazingly deep peace in spite of his circumstances. On the outside of things his life "sucks". This man is 24. He has no arms and no legs. When he was 8, he cried himself to sleep, saying, "Jesus, if you are real, why did you make me like this? When I wake up tomorrow, give me arms and legs." But he didn't get them. He grew up thinking he could never get married or have children or that if he did, he would never be able to hold or touch them. What a bleak prospect for anyone to face. But this man, who admits he has asked God every single question about security, peace and purpose, has learnt a deep inner contentment. He can now say, "I am fearfully and wonderfully made. Now, I wouldn't be any other way, because I am the person God has made me to be." Knowing the Prince of Peace has changed his life. He speaks with the wisdom of a 40-year old. He is so wise and utterly secure in Christ.

I don't tell you this to make you feel ashamed. It is not helpful to compare our situation with someone else's and say it's "worse" or "not as bad". Everyone has their own cross to bear. What is bad for one is not necessarily bad for another. We all have issues to contend with and situations that threaten to steal our joy and rob us of our peace. If we are suffering, God knows and cares. He wants to bring us peace whether we are facing terminal cancer or a common cold.

His peace is available to everyone – the sick, the frightened and the lonely, the rich and the poor, the student and the billionaire. It may not change the circumstances of our lives.

We may never own a big car. We may remain single. We may not necessarily be healed of the disease we suffer from. But we can still know the tangible peace that surpasses human understanding. This peace is not on loan. We don't have to return it when we've finished with it, like some kind of dog-eared library book. It is a permanent, constant offer. To live at peace with God we must have our inner sin and our independence dealt with. We must allow Christ to be first in our lives. The Prince of Peace longs to reign on the throne of our hearts.

Thinking it through:

◊ What are you struggling with right now? What leads you to lose your peace?
◊ How secure are you? Are you constantly having to justify yourself to others?
◊ Do you crave people's attention and affirmation to the point where that might be unhealthy?
◊ Do you need "things" and possessions to bring you peace? And does that feeling fly away the minute you see the next thing you desire?
◊ What is it that brings offence in your life?

Take some time to come before the Prince of Peace and acknowledge who He is today. Offer Him the problems, fears and anxieties within that are threatening your inner stability. Ask Him to come and restore you.

> *"You may not understand the reason why I have you in this place right now, but I am setting you up for blessing and fruitfulness. The particular requirements I am placing upon you may not make sense to you or anyone else at this time.... But once you fully understand that these requirements will take you to a higher level – a place of peace, and a new path of destiny – you will follow without questioning."*[1]

---

1 Quote from Heaven Sent, Integrity Media Europe, 2009.

CHAPTER 11
Living Holiness

I wonder what type of person comes to your mind when I say the word "holy"? Is it someone you admire and want to be like, or someone you feel far removed from and unable to relate to?

Many of us have a view of holiness that is nothing like the biblical understanding. We see holiness as a dusty, dull word that we associate with someone quiet, staid and, if we are honest, slightly boring! We don't relate to the word with excitement, expectancy and enthusiasm.

I want to unpack, in this chapter, what I believe to be one of the most exhilarating, wonderful truths in Scripture – that we are called to be holy as God Himself is holy (Leviticus 19:2). An amazing and exciting God is asking us to become more like Him. What could possibly be boring about that?

When Jesus went into a town, the people of all ages flocked to Him. Jesus was the holiest man to ever walk the earth and people just wanted to surround Him and be like Him. I want to be that type of person for God too – a person who is characterised by living holiness – a person who attracts others to the Father. What about you?

What is Living Holiness?

Living holiness is one of the lovely phrases used in the Free Methodist Church. But what does it really mean?

The Hebrew word for holiness is *kadash* which means to "set apart or distinguish from the ordinary". In New Testament Greek the word for holy *hagios* means "separate from common use and reserved or sanctified for special use".

To be holy, then, means to be unlike the ordinary, to stand out and be separate from others. It means to be clean ceremonially and morally, to be consecrated and laid on one side for God's use and purposes. True holiness like this is life-giving, life-fulfilling and life-gaining. It is all about how we can live life to the full.

Mother Teresa said: "True holiness consists of doing God's will with a smile."

What is "dead" holiness?

I was brought up to believe that holiness was all about what you *didn't* do. I view this as a "dead" and lifeless holiness. When I was a little boy, our church Sunday school offered a special badge called the "Lord's Day Observance Badge". It's true! If anyone bought sweets on the way to church, or broke the rules of the Sabbath, we were encouraged to tell the superintendent. The person who had transgressed then had their badge taken away and the person who had told on them was given an extra one. I thought this was holiness!

We were given a whole list of things we couldn't do. As boys, we couldn't watch live rugby, go to the cinema, drink or smoke, wear hats in church or buy anything on a Sunday. Girls had to wear hats; no makeup or attractive clothes were allowed.

We were told to come to the midweekly prayer meeting, to attend church twice every Sunday and, if we were bored, we could always fast! Does that kind of lifestyle appeal to you? Me neither! It's a wonder we had any Christians in the church at that time!

Those who taught us thought that to enjoy oneself was against the call to holiness. I have learnt since that holiness is not a deprivation of things or some legalistic list of "do's" and "don'ts". Holiness isn't: I don't go there, I don't say that, I don't watch that. That's not living! Living holiness is not achieved by refraining from a list of prohibited activities or fearing threats of God's displeasure. Holiness isn't: "If I do this I'm damned ... it's *I want to do this because I'm redeemed!"*

We don't seek to discipline our children by threatening them, do we? That isn't love, that's fear. My God is coming back as a Bridegroom to collect His Bride. He does not want us to live as though we're frightened of Him. Holiness is provoked by God's love, mercy and compassion, not by fear of His judgement.

Therefore holiness cannot be achieved by Law but by living in His grace. Holiness comes from the greatest commandment: "You shall love the Lord your God with all your heart." We are His children and holiness is our natural response to that love.

Maybe some of us need to change the way we perceive holiness? Perhaps we see it as a restrictive, difficult thing that other people seem to do better at. In Matthew 11:29 - 30 Jesus says:

> *"Take my yoke up on you. Let me teach you, because I am humble and gentle at heart, and you will find rest for your souls. For my yoke is easy to bear, and the burden I give you is light."*
>
> NLT

Jesus speaks of being like Him in a gentle and easy, not difficult or demanding way. What's that got to do with legalistic holiness? Nothing!

How do we become holy?

As we all know, God is holy and relates only to holiness. He cannot be at one with a people who are unholy before Him. In fact, He demands that His people are holy:

> *"Speak to the entire assembly of Israel and say to them: 'Be holy because I, the LORD your God, am holy.'"*
> (Leviticus 19:2 NIV)

But He knows we are powerless to change the state we are in.

In Exodus 31:13 God speaks to Moses and says,

> *"Say to the Israelites, 'You must observe my Sabbaths. This will be a sign between me and you for the generations to come, so you may know that I am the LORD,* **who makes you holy.***"*
> NIV

It is God who makes us holy. It is nothing to do with who we are, what we know, how we dress or what we refrain from.

As 1 Peter 2:9 declares:

> *"But you are a chosen people, a royal priesthood, a holy nation, a people belonging to God, that you may declare the praises of him who called you out of darkness into his wonderful light."* NIV

Look at the characteristics named here:

◊ Chosen
◊ Royal
◊ Priesthood

- ◊ Holy
- ◊ Belonging to God
- ◊ Declaring Praises
- ◊ Out of darkness
- ◊ Into light

Real holiness is about being separated out for such blessings as these, not being separated *from* enjoyment. But notice that only one of these characteristics is about how *we* respond to God. The rest are about His love and compassionate blessings for us. Holiness is God's gift to His people. We are separated into the fullness not the emptiness of God!

We only have the ability to be holy through Christ, who has already become the sin offering for us, taking upon Himself the punishment of sin we deserve. Death entered into Him, so that we may qualify as holy before God.

In Exodus 15:11-13 Moses asks this question:

"Who is like You O LORD, among the gods?" NKJV

It's a great question, isn't it?

Look at the answers Moses then gives:

"Who is like you-majestic in holiness, awesome in glory, working wonders? You stretched out your right hand and the earth swallowed them. In your unfailing love you will lead the people you have redeemed. In your strength you will guide them to your holy dwelling." NIV

He is basically listing the qualities of the Holy God who enables him to come to the conclusion: no one is like you! God is unique in His holiness and calls us to live that unique and separate life too.

The characteristics of the holy person

So what do we need to be like in order to have this "living holiness" to the full?

- ***An awareness of holiness as God's gift***
As we have already discovered, holiness cannot be attained by a self-motivated or self-imposed pious lifestyle. True holiness is about living in the reality of the resurrected power of Jesus Christ. Holiness is not based on natural gifting. We can know the Word of God well and still not be holy. It's all about the Word of God knowing us. Ephesians 4:22-24 says:

> *"You were taught, with regard to your former way of life, to put off your old self, which is being corrupted by its deceitful desires; to be made new in the attitude of your minds; and to put on the new self, created to be like God in true righteousness and holiness."*
>
> NIV

Only God can help us be made new in this way so that we can be created like Him in true holiness.

- ***An awareness of holiness as a response***
Holiness is not the starting point for any human. It is a natural response to the power and majesty of God. We don't display holy living in order to be holy. God makes us holy and then a holy lifestyle and habits come naturally to us.
As Joseph Caryl says:
  "Perfect holiness is the aim of the saints on earth and it's the reward of the saints in heaven."

- ***An awareness of our humility before Him***

We don't achieve any level of holiness by acting a certain way. The Bible makes it clear that God has chosen us, not because we deserve His favour, but that we are nothing and lost without Him. As 1 Corinthians 1:27-30 (NIV) says:

> *"But God chose the foolish things of the world to shame the wise; God chose the weak things of the world to shame the strong. He chose the lowly things of this world and the despised things—and the things that are not—to nullify the things that are, so that no-one may boast before him. It is because of him that you are in Christ Jesus, who has become for us wisdom from God—that is, our righteousness, holiness and redemption."*

This verse means that we will never be humiliated by God. We may not merit His pardon and mercy, but He will never use that to treat us unkindly. His compassion for us is too great for that.

- ***A desire to be holy in how we think, live and speak.***

We cannot live a holy life if we think and act like the world. As it makes clear in Isaiah 6, we all need to have ourselves made clean and purified before God. Isaiah describes himself as a sinful man of "unclean lips" unable to do anything of worth for God. But after a burning coal is used to purge and clean his mouth, he is made fit to serve God. God speaks to Him and asks, "Whom shall I send?" Isaiah is able to say, "I will go! Send me!"

Now Jesus in the same way says: "Who will go for me?"

I want to be able to say: "I am clean! Send me!"

It's a pleasure to fulfil God's commands when we are seeking after holiness. We will love to please Him. It won't be a chore or a burden to us.

J.C. Ryle, the first Bishop of Liverpool, said:
"To commune with God in prayer, in the Bible, and in the assembly of His people – these things will be the holy man's chiefest enjoyments. He will value every thing and place and company, just in proportion as it draws him nearer to God."

- *Awareness that our holiness can be compromised by others*

The Bible speaks of not being unevenly yoked with non-believers (see 2 Corinthians 6:14). If we have a relationship in business, friendship or marriage that is unequal, we can begin to take on the other person's values and leave God's behind. The yoke begins to draw us away or drag us along at the wrong speed. But when a yoke is in God, it means we can pull together in the same direction at identical speed to achieve a common goal.

As it says in Mark 2:21:

> *"No-one sews a patch of unshrunk cloth on an old garment. If he does, the new piece will pull away from the old, making the tear worse."* NIV

In other words, we need to surround ourselves with like-minded, fellow believers in order to protect ourselves and stop us damaging ourselves and others.

- *Awareness that holiness needs constant work*

We won't ever achieve a state of perfect holiness. We will get things wrong from time-to-time. But the worst thing we can do is sit down and give up. We need to come to God in our weakness and repent of the ways in which we fail Him and don't live up to his holy standards. Hebrews 12:10 says:

"Our fathers disciplined us for a little while as they thought best; but God disciplines us for our good, that we may share in his holiness." NIV

How can we stay in a place of holiness?

Some things, only you can pray for yourself. The Bible says *you* have to put on the full armour of God (Ephesians 6:10). No one can put it on and wear it for you. We have a choice about whether or not to live a holy life. It is not up to our pastor, our partner or our friends.

How can we keep living a holy lifestyle?

There are some practical things I have learnt that you might find useful:

1 Don't allow things to remain in your life that remind you, and others, of what you used to be (James 1:21). You don't need them any more.

   For example, when we pray for someone to be released from an addiction to pornography, we challenge them to sort out their TV, their computer, the things they are reading and looking at and to get rid of those things.

2 Be transformed by the renewing of your mind (see Romans. 12:2). We become unholy because we are deluded that what we are doing is actually fulfilling us. But it becomes a lust that simply demands more. Being constantly renewed in our thinking and having a fresh mental and spiritual attitude means we are more likely not to fall into bad habits.

3 Don't ever let your anger last after the sun goes down (Ephesians 4:26). If you go to bed angry, it solidifies in the soul. Don't give the devil an opportunity to enter your thinking. If you have harmed or upset someone, seek to be reconciled with them. There is such a thing in the Bible as the doctrine of restoration, but not many preach it today. I believe that if you have spent a life thieving and cheating, your first responsibility, when you are born

again, is to give back what you have taken. Take a leaf out of Zacchaeus' book. We are told in Luke 19:8 that,

"Zacchaeus stood up and said to the Lord, 'Look, Lord! Here and now I give half of my possessions to the poor, and if I have cheated anybody out of anything, I will pay back four times the amount.'"

NIV

In Jewish Law, if you had cheated someone you were asked to pay back four times that amount. But look what Zacchaeus' new-found holiness required his heart to do in addition. He willingly chooses to give half his money to the poor as well. What made him do that? It wasn't guilt. A new sense of purpose had flooded into his life.

4. Let no foul or polluting language come out of your mouth. Colossians 3:8 says,

"But now you must rid yourselves of all such things as these: anger, rage, malice, slander, and filthy language from your lips."

NIV

We have to stop being gossips and being negative and critical of other people. Every time we "bad-mouth" someone, we contaminate other people. We must say things that will progress and bless others.

Sometimes we do things in our lives that we can be forgiven for, but we can't put right. If we murder someone we can serve time for it, but we can't bring that person back. If we assassinate someone's character, it is often impossible to put that right as well.

I was once speaking at a wedding and the bride came down the aisle looking amazing. I thought to myself, "I must remember to say that she looks as pretty as a picture." What actually came out of my mouth though was, "She's no oil painting, is she?" I'd said it before I realised what I'd said and I couldn't then undo it. It was even recorded on their wedding video. Isn't that awful? Poor woman!

We must be careful what we say. Once it's out it's out.

The power of the holy person

Jesus said that the greatest prophet was John the Baptist. In Matthew 11:11 we read,

> *"I tell you the truth: Among those born of women there has not risen anyone greater than John the Baptist; yet he who is least in the kingdom of heaven is greater than he."*
>
> NIV

This is an extraordinary truth. We don't realise what power we have at our command. We've been born of the Spirit of God and by Him can do "all things through Christ". We can achieve amazing things for our incredible God when we realize who we are in Him.

I read a very moving letter recently from a lady dying of cancer. She had witnessed the holiness of a member of our church who lay dying in the same hospital ward. She chose to write a letter to Hazel's husband Ken, to tell him the impact Hazel had on her. Part of the letter reads like this:

"Dear Ken,

I knew her for just a few hours in hospital, but in that time, Hazel inspired me to get on with my life. She said, 'Don't let cancer dominate you.' Although she was in pain herself, she gave me hope and my faith was returned. She told me to trust in God to help me through any difficult time ahead of me ..."

Living holiness can even speak into that bleak situation. It is about a life separated. Even though Hazel was attached to all kinds of tubes and bloated by powerful steroids, she didn't forget Who she served.

Even in this terrible time of pain and death, Hazel was able to bring another person back into relationship with the Father. We have access to miracles of God no one has ever known.

Holiness like this gives us the strength to live as well as the courage to die. It's the kind of living holiness that I aspire to and that inspires me to wake up every morning full of energy to serve God.

Thinking it through:

"It is an undoubted truth that every doctrine that comes from God, leads to God; and that which does not tend to promote holiness is not of God." —George Whitefield

◊ How clean is your heart today?
◊ What are the areas of your life that the Holy Spirit is highlighting that you need to bring to Him again?
◊ Do you want to be someone who is not critical of others but known for speaking blessings? What do you need to do? Who do you need to start again with?

Maybe you would like to use this prayer and make it your own:

"Father God, I know that without You I can never be holy. Forgive the unholiness in my heart and in my spirit. Touch my lips with Your burning coal. Sanctify me and set me apart to achieve what You are calling me towards. I want to be made Holy to be used by You, Holy Lord. Amen."

CHAPTER 12 — Essential Truth

"I am truth"

Truth is not simply an attribute of Jesus, it's *who* He is. Jesus said:

> *"I am the way and the truth and the life. No-one comes to the Father except through me."*
>
> (John 14:6 NIV)

It would have been true if Jesus had said, "I'm great, I'm mighty and I'm fantastic." But He chose instead to give us three promises that we need in life and death. He didn't say, "I am *a* way", but "I am *the* way."

Notice that Jesus places "truth" in between "way" and "life". *He understood that if we mislay truth, we will lose our way and ultimately our very lives.* It is essential, then, that we grasp what truth is. Any man or woman who seeks Jesus must also seek to live in truth.

David saw this need to live a blameless life, characterised by truth:

> *"LORD, who may dwell in your sanctuary?*
> *Who may live on your holy hill?*
> *He whose walk is blameless*
> *and who does what is righteous,*
> *who speaks the truth from his heart."*
>
> (Psalm 15:1-2 NIV)

If we, as Christians, live in denial of His Word and our own sinfulness, then the truth is not in us (see 1 John 1:8). Sometimes our biggest problem is that we go to a good church every week and receive teaching, but we believe the message is meant for the person next to us!

Jesus speaks directly and truthfully to each of us about who He is and what He is about. I love this about Him. So often today people hedge their bets and give you a half-baked answer, don't they? Politicians seem to do this all the time. By mistake they tell you the truth occasionally – and then go back on it! But if you've got the courage to hear and face the truth of Jesus, you can build your life on it.

As a young man, full of frustration and anger, I found that so helpful. I like straight-talking people. So when I read that Jesus said, "I am the truth." I could understand that. The essence of real truth is not based on our understanding of morality, because this can differ according to our culture. Truth is nothing to do with living in your culture, which is a human interpretation; it's understanding Jesus' principles and purposes that counts.

So what is it that living in such truth offers us?

Truth brings knowledge

It's obvious to say that if you want to know somebody you have to spend time with them. 1 John puts it like this:

> "We know also that the Son of God has come and has given us understanding, so that we may know him who is true. And we are in him who is true—even in his Son Jesus Christ. He is the true God and eternal life."
>
> (1 John 5:20 NIV)

Unless you *know* Jesus you will struggle to hear Him or even recognize His voice from other voices.

When I was in the football business, there was a manager called Harry Haslam, the manager of Luton Town and Sheffield United – going back a few years. He was a real old-fashioned manager, a Northerner. He was a great guy, I really loved him, but every other word he said was a swearword.

Once, Harry recounted a conversation we'd had, to another manager who knew I was a Christian. Harry said, "I saw Dave Carr last week and he said he was so f*****g fed up that he can't b****y well cope with football today!"

The manager later said to me, "I know you would never have used those words." Why did the manager know I hadn't sworn? It was because he *knew* me.

When I was in Australia about ten years ago the Lord said to me, "Read just my words in the book of Matthew and when you've read them, come back to me." I had one of those Bibles that has the words of Jesus in red text, so I read through it for a couple of hours then went back to the Lord and said, "This is remarkable. The words in black only tell us where You were when You said it and the reaction of others. The words in red, your words, reveal YOU and Your truth. Lord, I'm embarrassed to say we don't preach them any more ..."

Do you know what the Lord said to me?

"Exactly."

So, for the next two years I just read and preached the words of Jesus. Though I'm not an expert, after two years of reading only Jesus, I can smell and hear if others use His words or not. I know what is true because truth is based on knowledge.

I remember saying to God that I wanted to preach a healing sermon and He said, "You start preaching my truths and let *Me* heal the sick. When you start getting the church into a righteous way, a way of truth and holiness, then you're going to see so many people healed that you won't know how to cope with it." He has proved true to His word.

Truth brings freedom

The Bible says in Psalm 51:6 that God desires truth in the inner parts. God isn't just interested in us being truthful "out loud", but also in our secret lives. Equally importantly in Isaiah it says,

> *"For truth is fallen in the street."*
> (Isaiah 59:14 NKJV)

There is no truth in the world any more. But surely there must be truth in Christians? Truth has the power to make us free. So if we're not free today, both inwardly "in the inner parts" and outwardly "on the street", we're not really living in truth.

> *"And you shall know the truth, and the truth shall make you free."*
> (John 8:32 NKJV)

Notice that it doesn't say "might" or "could", but *shall* make you free. If it's that simple, then why aren't we free? Because to tell the truth, to believe the truth, to hear the truth and to apply the truth can be very painful. We are not, by nature, truthful people.

People talk about white lies or half-truths. There is no such thing! Like white witches it's the same dirtiness painted another colour.

The Bible says that righteousness comes through faith and faith comes through the Word. The Bible says the same with truth:

> *"If you abide in My word, you are My disciples indeed."*
> (John 8:31 NKJV)

It's only those who abide who continue to dwell, endure, remain and stand in and on His word who will know the truth.

Jesus explains that sin makes us slaves and if we are a slave to sin then we serve unrighteousness. If we allow untruths in our lives and our mouths, and if we allow ourselves to develop close relationships with others who tell untruths, then we are slaves to unrighteousness. God says of people who do not live in the truth, they will:

> *"not abide in the house forever."*
> (John 8:35 NKJV)

This means a lack of truth will eventually evict you from the presence of God. Keep yourself surrounded at all times by truth. It will make you free!

Truth brings challenge

Isaiah 59:4 says,

> *"No one calls for justice, Nor does any plead for truth."* NKJV

People often say to me, "Pastor Dave, tell me the truth ...", inviting me to speak into their lives. There are times when I have to say to people, "You don't want truth; you can't take truth."

Five young men came to me some years ago and said, "Pastor Dave, we really want to go for God. Just tell us anything you see in us that will stop us. Tell us the truth." After I'd told them, three left immediately, one got sulky and the other left then eventually came back.

Christians are some of the worst people at accepting truth. If you can't be told the truth without getting offended you need to work on that! The truth shouldn't threaten or offend us. It sets us on the right track and puts things into their true perspective.

Pastor Chamberlain was a lovely man working in Dudley. He'd had a squint in one eye for years. Just before he retired I visited him and he'd frosted over one side of his glasses. I said, "What's wrong with your glasses, Gerald?" He said, "I led a young biker lad to the Lord and I said to him, 'Is there any question you want to ask?' He said, 'Yeah, which of your eyes do I look at?' "He's the only person who ever told me I had a problem with my eye, so I went and got it sorted."

Why did the church lie to him for so long? Surely that is cruel. The church sometimes can't cope with telling the truth. For example, why do we allow somebody who is a terrible musician to play the organ for twenty years and secretly mock her every week? A new pastor arrives and tells her the truth. Can you understand why she is so devastated? It's not just that she's been asked not to play, but because people have lied to her for twenty years.

The church can contain some of the biggest liars on the face of God's earth and yet we claim that we're Christians! Of course it can be costly to tell the truth, but we don't have to be offensive in our truthfulness, we can be compassionate as well as challenging. By us telling the truth, people can be healed. Obviously we don't just walk up and say, "You're ugly, you're fat, you're this or that …" That's not truth, that's rudeness. But truth is also about not lying; it's giving people a parameter of reality.

The husband of one of Molly's best friends was taken ill and went to hospital. The doctor said, "You've got tumours in both lungs." His wife asked, "Excuse me doctor, what does that mean?"

"Well, it's not good," the doctor responded.

"Is he going to die?"

"Well, aren't we all going to die, Mrs Bickerstaff?"

"But when?"

"Who knows? He could be knocked over tomorrow."

They ended up in my office. He said, "I just don't know what to do. What's happening to me? I've got tumours in both lungs."

"Are they going to give you radium?" I asked.

"No."

"Are they going to give you chemo?"

"No, the doctor just said to go home and enjoy my family."

I said, "Well, if you've got a tumour in one lung they can take it out, but you can't live without two lungs. If they're not giving you any treatment Barry, then you're going to die."

He looked at me and said, "Do you know how long?"

I said, "I'm no doctor but I reckon six to eight months maximum." (I only said this because I've dealt with sick people all my life).

He started weeping.

I said, "I'm sorry to have upset you, but you did want the truth."

He said, "No, no, I'm just weeping because I've been so worried. Nobody would tell me the truth. Now I know, I can get myself sorted out."

I said, "Why have you never got born again?"

He said, "Somebody told me once that a Christian must read the Bible every day and I can't read."

I said, "No, the Bible has to read *you* everyday. I'll give you a set of tapes and you can listen to it."

He got thoroughly born again and the week before he died he was sitting there with a Bible in his lap. His wife said to him, "What are you doing? You can't read."

He said, "Yes I can!" God had done a miracle for him.

Never ask me for the truth because you'll get it! When you love people you never lie. Don't ever lie to your wife, or your husband, your children or your friends. Truth is challenging but it's also healing!

Truth brings an eternal perspective

Abraham Lincoln told the story of an Eastern Monarch who wanted a lasting legacy to be written where generations of people would see it. He asked his wisest advisers to come up with a sentence that would always be true, no matter what was happening in the world or the kingdom at that time. They presented him with six words:

"And this, too, shall pass away".

This King wanted a truth that, regardless of what they would discover in the future, would always be true. That's quite profound, isn't it?

The only thing that will not pass away is truth. It's who Jesus is, what He is and what He does. The Bible is clear that the reign of Jesus will never end. He is the way of truth leading into eternity.

Galileo said,

"All truths are easy to understand once they are discovered; the point is to discover them."

All truth is easy; the hardest thing is finding what truth is. Once you have found Jesus, your searching is over. You have found TRUTH!

They don't teach you to do a wedding or a funeral at most Theological Colleges. They teach you theology and then throw you into a church. When students come to our church now, one of the things I do with them is take them to the undertakers. They're shown a dead body laid out and see all that happens to that person. I believe that if they don't see this before they have to conduct a funeral then they'll want to run when they're needed. They actually thank me for it.

As a pastor I want to be there when people die. I want to hold them when they go! I've had lots of people die in my arms. I've helped lay them out. I've picked them up and put them in the box. What use would I be as a pastor if I was hiding under the table?

When you understand the eternal perspective of truth you are able to do these things. Jesus is truth now as much as He was when He was on earth. Understanding that brings great depth to life.

Now, if Jesus is the way and the truth then He gives us life and, according to Him, it doesn't actually end at death but catapults itself into a new expression.

"Change and decay in all around I see:
O thou who changest not, abide with me"
(Abide With Me, Henry Francis Lyte)

Proverbs 14:12 says,

"There is a way that seems right to a man, but its end is the way of death." NKJV

Note that, without truth, man misses life and engages death. If we don't find the truth of life and the truth of God, then we find death because only God can take us to life.

The English Revised Version puts the emphasis on the ways of death. This can mean not just a final separation from God, but death in many walks of our life. How many of us have found, through broken truth, that our relationships have gone, our businesses have folded up, our church fellowship has collapsed and marriages are on the rocks? Even our health, both physical and mental, can suffer because somewhere down the line there hasn't been truth.

Truth brings change

As Christians we should manifest truth in every area of our lives. We should live it, talk it, hear it and write it. Look at these verses about different aspects of living:

> *"Lead me in Your truth and teach me, for You are the God of my salvation;"*
>
> (Psalm 25:5 NKJV)

> *"I have chosen the way of truth ..."*
>
> (Psalm 119:30 NKJV)

> *"And take not the word of truth utterly out of my mouth."*
>
> (Psalm 119:43 NKJV)

If someone's prepared to tell you the truth don't you dare bite their head off for doing it! If you ask your husband to tell the truth and he does, but then you won't speak to him for a week, that just isn't godly.

Those of us who are parents need to consider this very carefully. How can we teach children anything if we don't tell the truth? How can you punish a child for lying, when you lie? Every child hears lies. They hear us lie on the phone, they hear us criticise people in church and then meet them in the doorway and be nice to them. Then, when the child lies to you, you get angry with them! It's true, isn't it? Children can lie without you teaching them, but actually, mainly they lie because they watch and mimic you and me.

My three-year-old granddaughter came up to me the other week and said, "I love you, Grandad."

I said, "I love you too, poppet."

She said, "You're weird ..."

She was telling the truth! I'm as nutty as a fruitcake. She understands that.

We need to reward our children when they speak the truth and not act like this:

"Tell me child, did you take that cake?"

"Yes."

SLAP!

Why would that little girl ever tell you the truth again? I'm not advocating rewarding children for sinning, but the punishment must now be different because they've told the truth. It should be nothing like as bad.

It's painful to receive the truth, painful to tell the truth, but I tell you this: we need to live as people who don't lie by our actions and deeds, or by our silence. Sometimes you can actually lie by not saying anything and by allowing someone to badmouth, to be bitter, rude and horrible while you just sit there and don't enter into the conversation. If you were telling the truth you'd say, "Stop that! You're talking about my friend ... my wife ... my church ... Now be quiet! You shouldn't say that because you won't say it to the person themselves."

Only Jesus said, "I'm truth. I'm the only way and I'm the life." Jesus tells you the truth. This means that every promise He makes is also true. He will never go back on His word. Aren't you glad that God tells you the truth?

We need to say, "God, I want to walk in truth, not lies. Your Word is truth!" We need to get into the Word of God because this will bring true change in us.

Truth brings judgement

John 17:17 says:

> *"Sanctify them by Your truth. Your word is truth. As You sent Me into the world, I also have sent them into the world. And for their sakes I sanctify Myself, that they also may be sanctified by the truth."*
> (John 17:17-19 NKJV)

Truth is not an option. We can't be selective about whether we're going to tell the truth. We're not going to be selective if we live in truth. We can't, each day, select truth. To disbelieve the truth and reject it places us on a collision course with God and with His provision. Romans 1:18 says,

> *"For the wrath of God is revealed from heaven against all ungodliness and unrighteousness of men, who suppress the truth in unrighteousness,"* NKJV

Romans 2:2 says,

> *"But we know that the judgment of God is according to truth against those who practice such things."* NKJV

God will not judge us according to how much money we've got and how much good we've done. He will judge us against the person and truth of Jesus. He will judge us according to what we've done with Christ.

In Romans 2:8 He says,

> *"But to those who are self-seeking and do not obey the truth, but obey unrighteousness—indignation and wrath."* NKJV

He put it this way in verse 20,

> "... an instructor of the foolish, a teacher of babes, having the form of knowledge and truth in the law."
> NKJV

Romans 2:21 says,

> "You, therefore, who teach another, do you not teach yourself? You who preach that a man should not steal, do you steal?"
> NKJV

Just because we go to church, put our hands in the air and sing and put our money in the offering, that doesn't make us Christian. Truth must be reflected in the words we speak and in our actions.

How do we act towards each other? How easy do we find it to forgive each other?

Truth does not rejoice in iniquity, but rejoices in itself. It bears all things and believes all things. I'm not a naïve man; I'm not stupid. I might look it and act it, but I'm not. Nevertheless, I believe people. I'm trying to be what Christ would want me to be. Because God doesn't lie, whatever He says is truth. Jesus promised to send the Spirit of truth in John 14:16-17:

> "And I will pray the Father, and He will give you another Helper, that He may abide with you forever— the Spirit of truth, whom the world cannot receive, because it neither sees Him nor knows Him; but you know Him, for He dwells with you and will be in you."
> NKJV

The Spirit of truth, if we commit our lives to Christ, lives in us so we should be able to discern between truth and lies.

> *"But when the Helper comes, whom I shall send to you from the Father, the Spirit of truth who proceeds from the Father, He will testify of Me."*
>
> (John 15:26 NKJV)

> *"However, when He, the Spirit of truth, has come, He will guide you into all truth; for He will not speak on His own authority, but whatever He hears He will speak; and He will tell you things to come."*
>
> (John 16:13 NKJV)

So the Spirit of truth tells us what's going to happen in our future and tells us what's going to happen when we die. We're all going to die eventually. Father, Son and Holy Spirit are truth. The Lord is looking for those who will worship him in Spirit and truth:

> *"But the hour is coming, and now is, when the true worshipers will worship the Father in spirit and truth; for the Father is seeking such to worship Him. God is Spirit, and those who worship Him must worship in spirit and truth."*
>
> (John 4:23-24 NKJV)

God is looking for people who want to know the truth. Only in Christ Jesus do we hear the defining declaration, "I am the way to the Father; I am the only truth for humanity; I am the only life for the dying."

Is He not the very essence of truth?

Truth brings self-awareness

Truth brings sincerity. When you get to the point where you're living God's truth, you actually begin to know who you are. You may think that if anyone thinks something bad of you then you must be what they say. But a really secure man or woman, if they know who they are, does not have to defend themselves. You are able to live at peace with yourself.

When my mother-in-law was dying, my son went to visit her. He noticed the most hideous looking vase in her home. It was orange and blue, yellow, red and green. Because her mind was going he said, "Nan, where did you get that?"

"I've always had it," she said. (What happened in her life was that anytime a neighbour threw something out, she'd be given it).

My son's an artist and he thought this vase looked familiar. So he went to the library to check the pattern. On discovering that it was a Clarice Cliff, he took it to be valued.

The valuer said, "Hmmm, I don't think you'll get more than £2000 – £3000 for this ..." My Son was a starving student! Nan had never had £3,000 in her life. She'd been sitting on something that nobody knew the value of.

Jesus looks at our life in much the same way. He walks in and thinks, "I recognise that pattern. I see the value in that person." He knows what it's like to have a broken body, a broken spirit and heart. He knows what it is for you to be fighting sickness, despair and loneliness.

Let me tell you what truth does to you. The story is told that, in an oriental bazaar where pottery was displayed in a dimly lit room, unscrupulous merchants would patch up the cracked pottery and rub it with wax to disguise the fact. But an intelligent buyer, knowing this might be the case, would hold up the pottery in the sun to judge its quality. He could see if there were any cracks. When you hold Jesus up to the light, you see the truth of who He is and who you are. He brings a transparency, a genuine purity and an unsoiled innocence.

So isn't it worth telling the truth? Isn't it worth receiving the truth? Isn't it worth living in truth? When you live in that truth you never have to fear a lie coming back to haunt you because you'll always have it told as it is.

If He's the truth then He's also the life, and if He's the life, He's also the way. When He says, "Come to me if you're heavy laden and I will give you rest," then He will. And if He says, "They that call upon the name of the Lord shall be saved," then they are.

More of God, more truth; that's what we all need!

Some people need to tell the truth for the first time and say, "God, I actually need you." He won't turn around and say, "Oh, it's all very well you saying that now …" He'll say, "I know. Here I am." Until you ask Him, He can't do anything. Until you seek Him, you can't find Him and until you knock, the door to His blessing can't be opened.

A truthful man and woman go to bed at night and never have to worry about what they've said during the day. Wouldn't it be wonderful when you take your last breath to not have to worry what you've said to God because He already knows?

Truth refutes lies
James 3:14 says this,

> *"do not boast and lie against the truth"*   NKJV

because when you boast you're exaggerating and this is not the truth. James 5:19 also talks about those who wander from the truth. Once you've found the truth, it only makes you free as long as you stay in it. It's so easy to drift away from the truth. If knowing truth makes us free, what happens if we choose to believe a lie? What happens if we won't submit to truth? 2 Thessalonians 2:11 says,

> *"And for this reason God will send them strong delusion, that they should believe the lie."* NKJV

Some people have got to the stage in their life where they wouldn't believe the truth if it slapped them in the face.

> *"When the wicked one appears, Satan will pretend to work all kinds of miracles, wonders, and signs. Lost people will be fooled by his evil deeds. They could be saved, but they will refuse to love the truth and accept it. So God will make sure that they are fooled into believing a lie. All of them will be punished, because they would rather do evil than believe the truth."*
> (2 Thessalonians 2:9-12 CEV)

It's saying here, that people are given an opportunity to believe truth, but they would rather accept a lie.

When I was involved in football I'd go to a player and say, "This is how much you will get in your current contract and that's how much you can get if you transfer. If we do all that work for you it will cost you about £2,000." But then an agent would come along and often tell the player a pack of lies and charge him £40,000. The footballer would say to me, "I've gone with him, Dave, because he must be able to get me more as he's charging me £40,000." The truth was that we weren't ripping him off and would get him the same contract! One footballer came to us once and said, "But this agent has given me a top of the range answer-phone ..." So my mate Brian said to him, "Take care of that because, if it cost you £30,000 in agent's fees, then it's the most expensive answer-phone you'll ever own." The footballer looked at him and suddenly the alarm bells started ringing. People sometimes choose a lie because the lie seems more attractive than reality. It never occurred to these guys that if their agent drove a Ferrari, somebody must have bought it for him!

Thinking it through:

> *"He is the Rock, His work is perfect;*
> *For all His ways are justice,*
> *A God of truth and without injustice;*
> *Righteous and upright is He."*
>
> (Deuteronomy 32:4 NKJV)

George Orwell said this:

> *"In a time of universal deceit — telling the truth is a revolutionary act."*

◊ Is God speaking to you about the lack of truth in your life?

◊ Do you want to know His truth in the inner part of you and know the truth about who you are?

◊ Do you want God to help you live in His truth? Perhaps you could dwell on the words of this prayer.

"Jesus, I want to thank you that You don't just tell the truth; You are the truth. Please reveal Your Word of truth to me. Let the Bible become so real to me that I meet Your truth on every page.

Lord, I want to be truthful in all my ways. In the way I speak, in the way I think, in the way I react and in the way I walk. I want to be truthful and I want people to be truthful with me.

I want to tell the truth and, if others reject me or what I say, Lord I forgive them because I've been there. I've been in a place where I couldn't take truth. But I want to know the truth that will make me free.

I want the truth in my inner person. That's who I am and that's who I am going to be. By the power of Your Spirit, Amen."

CHAPTER 13
Divine Compassion

> *"Your attitude should be the same as that of Christ Jesus: Who, being in very nature God, did not consider equality with God something to be grasped, but made himself nothing, taking the very nature of a servant, being made in human likeness."*
>
> (Philippians 2:5-7 NIV)

The Jesus you and I serve chose to make Himself *nothing* and become a servant for us. He was made in "human likeness" in order that He might truly know and share in all our experiences – our joys *and* our sufferings. He was both divine and yet human. These two aspects of His nature allow Him to be a God of deep compassion. There is no emotion, circumstance or situation outside His unfathomable love, mercy and grace.

I pray that as you read this chapter you will meet with the Jesus of divine compassion, the Jesus who portrayed servanthood in every way, so that you and I could know the depths of God's acceptance.

Revelation leads to compassion

In Exodus 33:12-21 we read the amazing story of Moses speaking with God about His presence and His compassion. Moses says:

> *"If you are pleased with me, teach me your ways so I may know you and continue to find favour with you... The LORD replied, 'My Presence will go with you, and I will give you rest.' Then Moses said to him, 'If your Presence does not go with us, do not send us up from here ... What else will distinguish me and your people from all the other people on the face of the earth?' And the LORD said to Moses, 'I will do the very thing you have asked, because I am pleased with you and I know you by name.' Then Moses said, 'Now show me your glory."* NIV

Why did Moses ask to see God's glory and not His face or His hands? The request Moses makes was not a desire to see God in human form. The clue here is in what this word "glory" actually signifies. The Hebrew word used here means abundance, wealth, treasure, majesty and splendour. Moses wanted to see God's awesomeness. He wanted a revelation of God's character.

This is what the LORD replied:

> *"'I will cause all my goodness to pass in front of you, and I will proclaim my name, the LORD, in your presence. I will have mercy on whom I will have mercy, and I will have compassion on whom I will have compassion. But, he said, 'you cannot see my face, for no-one may see me and live."*

God says here that He will cause all His *goodness*, His mercy, His compassionate love, to pass in front of Moses. What a sight and sensation that must have been! God is full of goodness and compassion. They are at the very heart of His character and DNA. Both His goodness and mercy pursue us as David says in Psalm 23. His goodness and compassion want to be where we are. I honestly believe that we can't be Christians without experiencing the goodness, mercy and divine compassion of God.

Notice also in this verse that God says He will "proclaim His name, the Lord" in Moses' presence. What is the significance of this? The Bible teaches us that the name of the LORD is a strong tower, a place that people can run to and be safe (see Proverbs 18:10). The value of God's compassion is based on the value of His name. It's a bit like a cheque, if it is not signed then the person will not be paid. A cheque is only as good as the credit or name of the payer. Similarly, you can know the name of the LORD as your strong tower today.

God's heart of compassion

Micah 7:19 says,

> *"You will again have compassion on us; you will tread our sins underfoot and hurl all our iniquities into the depths of the sea."* NIV

God's nature is to have compassion on His people. This is His default setting. Notice that Micah says, *"You will again ..."* In other words, this is not a one-off agreement. God chooses to treat us in this way, time and time again. This verse teaches us that He actively tramples our sins under His feet and then throws them into the deepest part of the oceans. What does this tell us about God's attitude to the things we do wrong? His desire is to quash them, remove their power and then throw them somewhere we cannot retrieve them!

The King James version uses these powerful words:

> *"He will **subdue** all our iniquities."*

In other words, He will restrain them, suppress them and bring them into captivity. Don't we need that subduing in some areas of our lives? Aren't you glad that you have a God who understands that need in your life? I know I am!

It's true that some of the battles we face in life don't leave us after we pray one prayer. But we have a God who understands that and journeys through that process with us. Maybe you have known struggles with alcohol in your life and, although people have prayed with you often, it is still an ongoing struggle? Perhaps you are facing a long-term health problem and have had ministry but have seen no change in your condition? The word that God says to you today is this:

"I will again have compassion on you, I will tread those problems of yours under My feet and hurl them as far away from you as I can. And remember, because I am God, that means very much further than *you* could ever throw them!"

True worship leads to true compassion

Compassion can be defined as a human emotion, prompted by the pain or anguish of others. It is more vigorous than empathy; it's not just a sense of "I really feel for you" and being able to sympathise with someone. Compassion is much more powerful than this. It is the deep awareness of the suffering of another, coupled with the active desire to relieve it.

Obviously you don't have to be a Christian to be a person of compassion. I served in the St. John's Ambulance when I was younger. In the old days, we could even respond to 999 calls would you believe? We had exactly the same training as ambulance staff. It was a messy job, but we were privileged to see some really amazing things. We didn't get paid, but it was incredibly rewarding. Lots of people who did that job with me weren't Christians, but they had real compassion and wanted to relieve the suffering of those in distress.

I find it hard to envisage being a Christian but *not* having compassion. I travel frequently and something people often say to me is, "Dave, you have such a heart for others." But rather than finding this a compliment, it worries me. It should be common to *all* who profess to be Christians, not just a few. People shouldn't comment on it in me, because they should be able to see it in *everyone* who bears the name of Christ. Sadly, there isn't much compassion around, not even in the Body of Christ where it should abound! We must all guard against becoming so high-tech in our Churches that we forget about caring for *people*.

To be compassionate is to be full of grace and mercy towards others, no matter who they are. We can't be proud and compassionate at the same time. Those things just don't mix. To treat someone with compassion means that we have to bend and stoop in kindness to someone in an inferior situation. There is no room for pride in that! Maybe for someone greater, we would find it easier to serve? Perhaps we would be quick to say, "Guess what I did for the boss today?" or "Look what such and such asked *me* to do." But this is not the heart of compassion at all. Showing true compassion often demands a sacrifice and a level of being inconvenienced.

I find it interesting that the definition of worship is so similar to the true meaning of compassion. Worship means to "bow down, to bend and stoop and kiss." I don't think we can learn to offer ourselves in compassion until we have bent and offered ourselves in worship.

We all know our place before the throne of God. We are all inferior before Him. None of us is worthy. And yet He allows us to approach. True worship and true compassion go together – they are not separate. When we have our wills broken by our Father, our hearts can be broken for His people. So if you want to be compassionate, learn first to worship. Learn to *look up* in worship and He will teach you to *look out* in compassion.

Living compassionately

Once I was invited somewhere incredibly prestigious. I was given the honour of joining the Bishop of Birmingham as he was installed as Archbishop of York. Due to the fact that my wife Molly was ill and couldn't join me, I went alone. It was a fascinating glimpse into the world of the top-ranking bishops and dignitaries of the Church of England. All day, I had Bishops coming up to me, thinking they'd gone a bit senile, asking, "Remind me which diocese you serve in?" When I told them, "I am a Methodist", they looked quite shocked. The fact that I was there at all was a bit of a surprise – to them and to me!

On the way to the meal at the Lord Mayor of London's Mansion House, the Bishop of Birmingham spotted a young female curate who used to be on his staff. He asked her if she was married and she replied that she was not. He turned to me and said, "As your wife wasn't able to come, why don't you two go in together?" She went beetroot red, but smiled and agreed to join us (she was only in her twenties so it must have looked a little odd to people as we arrived!). When we got through the door, I turned to her, declared our short-lived "marriage" annulled and then released her to go and enjoy herself!

This is a small picture of what godly compassion is like. It takes us in off the street and puts us in a place we don't deserve to be. It gives us status as His children, and belonging, as members of His family. Compassion invites us into community.

The practical outworking of compassion

Imagine being present at Jesus' transfiguration! (see Matthew 17). No one had ever seen the picture of Jesus that Peter, James and John were allowed to witness. They saw Him, not just as human, but as God for the first time. We are told in verse 6 that they were terrified and fell face down to the ground. It must have been an incredible, awesome sight.

> *"There he was transfigured before them. His face shone like the sun, and his clothes became as white as the light. Just then there appeared before them Moses and Elijah, talking with Jesus."*
>
> (Matthew 17:2-3 NIV)

The disciples then come down the mountain, having seen this amazing miracle and bump into a distraught man. He cries that his son, possessed by a demon, keeps throwing himself into fire and water to try and kill himself. He begs the three disciples to heal and release the boy, but they are unable to help the man. How extraordinary! They have just spent time gazing at the very presence and glory of the transfigured Christ, together with men who summed up the Law and the prophets! Now, when called upon, they cannot help this stranger. You would think that this revelation would have stirred both their faith and their compassion levels to a new high!

Jesus was incredulous at their lack of trust, and spoke harshly to them,

> *"You faithless and corrupt people! How long must I be with you? How long must I put up with you?"*
> (Matthew 17:17 NLT)

I find myself feeling like this sometimes about the Church. There are occasions when I just want to shout at people: "Don't tell me how well you speak in tongues or how many people were healed at your church last week! Don't tell me how good your sermons are or how many prophecies you have ... if you have no compassion for your fellow man, it's all worthless!" I really believe that, if you turn away someone in need, you haven't really had a revelation of who Jesus is at all. His divine compassion needs to impact us to be people of divine compassion too.

Mother Teresa was once taking pus from a leper's leg. The commentator with her said in a horrified voice, "I could never do that!" She turned to him briefly and said, "No, neither could I." Do you get what she was saying? She was saying that without the compassion of Christ, she was unable to be compassionate in the way she needed to be.

Sometimes we ask God for a miracle. We ask for a sign that He is there. But maybe He says back to us, "What's the point in revealing Myself to you, if you do what the disciples did and come down the mountain and completely ignore those I bring to you." God's revelation must lead to our re-imagining the world around us. That is the whole point of Him revealing who He is!

At the church I pastor, we try to put divine compassion into practical action in many ways. If people are struggling with debt, we have a free service in partnership with *Christians Against Poverty* (see www.CAPUK.org) which offers a debt counselling service. If a person comes to us with a broken window or some kind of work needed in their home, we have a maintenance team who will work free of charge to bless that person. If people come to us hungry, we have a food programme – if they are not too proud to accept it. We will even teach people to read and access important documents and information, if that is what they require. But we do it free. Compassion is costly to the giver, but not to the receiver.

George Washington Carver said, "How far you go in life depends on your being tender with the young, compassionate with the aged, sympathetic with the striving and tolerant of the weak and strong. Because someday in your life you will have been all of these."

Receiving Jesus' compassion from Him and from others

What stuns me about the Jesus we serve is that He also longs to serve us. He chooses to wash our feet, to give to us all we need; and yet sometimes we have the audacity to say to Him, "Look at *my* church, *my* ministry, *my* gifting" as if it belongs to us! If Jesus chose not to serve us, we wouldn't have anything with which to serve Him!

This all powerful Jesus is gracious and has pity on us. He chooses to bend and stoop down to our level. Often our pride gets in the way, doesn't it? We can find it hard to receive what He longs to give us. This can also be the case with others. What do you do when people offer to bless you? Are you quick to take offence and think, "I can cope on my own thank you! How dare you offer me anything!" or, are you able to thank and bless them for their willingness to serve you?

I can remember in the early days of my being a pastor, we were too poor to buy a carpet for our floor. We wouldn't go into debt for it, so I said to Molly that I would have to go out and work for it another way. She reminded me that I had promised not to do that and that we would trust God for His provision.

One day, a couple from the church rang up. The husband had a high-powered job at a local water company. They had inherited some money and wanted to tithe it. When they prayed about this, God told them to pay for us to have some new carpet. So they rang me and made the offer.

"Do you need some carpet, Pastor Dave?"

"Well, I may do," I said nonchalantly, thinking, "Please don't offer me charity!"

They repeated the offer.

"I couldn't accept that," I said. (At this point, I had Molly in the background frantically waving at me, mouthing, "Say yes! Say yes!")

I am good at giving things away, but I wasn't good at receiving things! I kept thinking, "There are people, poorer than I am, with more needs than I have." So I said this to the couple. They replied, "Yes, we know that, but God said that He wanted to teach you a lesson!" They also told me I had a ceiling of money that I wasn't allowed to spend UNDER! I had to bite my lip and agree! So we chose a lovely carpet and had it laid and fitted. You would think I learnt my lesson from this. But no!

A few weeks later we were due to have someone round for lunch. Molly came to me and said, "Dave, we have no potatoes. What am I going to do?" I didn't have any answers or any money. Later that morning in church, a very wealthy and well-spoken lady came up to me. "Pastor Dave," she said, "I was doing my devotions this morning and I read the passage about bringing the first fruits to the priest. I looked out into my garden and saw that I hadn't yet harvested the potatoes. I felt God telling me to bring you these." Then she handed me a large bag of potatoes. I got home and gave them to Molly joking, "All we need now is a big steak, Mol!" I opened the front door a little while later and found one on the doorstep. I felt God saying to me, "Have you learnt yet? Those who give compassion must also learn to receive it from Me and from others."

I have never forgotten that simple lesson.

Think of what Jesus said to Peter when he complained about Jesus washing his feet in John 13:5-8:

> *"After that, he poured water into a basin and began to wash his disciples' feet, drying them with the towel that was wrapped around him. He came to Simon Peter, who said to him, 'Lord, are you going to wash my feet?' Jesus replied, 'You do not realise now what I am doing, but later you will understand.' 'No,' said Peter, 'you shall never wash my feet.' Jesus answered, 'Unless I wash you, you have no part with me."* NIV

These are stark words, aren't they? "Unless I wash you, you have *no* part with me." Jesus is making it clear to Peter and to us, "If you don't let Me serve you, you don't share My nature, My DNA." To serve Christ is to also allow ourselves to be served by Him.

We were once invited to go to New Zealand and speak at a few churches. Another friend of ours had warned us that the church out there did not know how to bless people and that we would end up paying heavily from our own pocket for the trip, but we still felt it was right to go. They paid my airfare and I paid Molly's. It was our wedding anniversary whilst we were out there, so we wanted to be together.

We prayed for the sick wherever we went and had a wonderful few days of ministry. Whilst we were there, one of the pastors asked us if we had any connections in that part of the world. I told them that Molly had an Aunt who lived in Napier and I had a nephew who lived in Christchurch.

The next day, in a prayer meeting, Molly received a phone call saying that they had bought us tickets to fly to Napier to see her Aunt. Two days later, my nephew rang the hotel to say that we had been given plane tickets to fly and see him also!

Later in the trip, we had planned one day off and were meant to be staying with a pastor and his wife. But they dropped us off at the Raffles Hotel in Wellington. I thought there must be some mistake, but the pastor replied, "No mistake. It's your wedding anniversary tomorrow, isn't it? You can have the best of everything." We had an incredible room and a beautiful meal.

I went down the following day to pay the bill at Reception, but was told it had been paid three months earlier! Then we were taken to the airport and given a brown envelope which contained all the money for Molly's airfare! I asked, "Why have you been so generous to us? Why have you done all this for me?" The man replied, "You are the only preacher we have ever had who took time to pray with every single person at the meetings, not just the first five. You stayed until the weakest and frailest had also made the effort to come forward. And you never asked us for anything in return. So we wanted to bless you."

When we got home, I shared this story of God's amazing generosity with our friend and he stood with his mouth open. I don't share this in any way to glorify myself, but to show what happens when we step out with compassionate faith.

The compassion of Christ

Jesus has all the compassion of the Father. He has inherited that same power in His name. Philippians 2:9 says,

> *"Therefore God exalted him to the highest place and gave him the **name that is above every name**."* NIV

Why is it that Christians can behave so badly at times? Why can we be so rude and arrogant, so quick to take offence? We see Jesus' goodness pass before us every day in terms of His blessing and favour, and yet we do not pass that on to others. We need to truly experience the compassion of Christ in order to show it to those around us. We need to remember that His name is above every other name – including and especially our own!

Jesus showed us divine compassion in many different circumstances in the Gospels. Just look at these instances of where He demonstrates it or speaks of it:

- *"When he saw the crowds, he had compassion on them, because they were harassed and helpless, like sheep without a shepherd."*

(Matthew 9:36 NIV)

- *"Come to me, all you who are weary and burdened, and I will give you rest."*

(Matthew 11:28 NIV)

- *"Soon afterward, Jesus went to a town called Nain, and his disciples and a large crowd went along with him. As he approached the town gate, a dead person was being carried out—the only son of his mother, and she was a widow. And a large crowd from the town was with her. When the Lord saw her, his heart went out to her and he said, 'Don't cry.'"*

(Luke 7:11-13 NIV)

- *"But a Samaritan, who was on a journey, came upon him; and when he saw him, he felt compassion."*

(Luke 10:33, NASB)

- *"But while he was still a long way off, his father saw him and was filled with compassion for him; he ran to his son, threw his arms around him and kissed him."*
  (Luke 15:20 NIV)

- *"When Jesus landed and saw a large crowd, he had compassion on them and healed their sick."*
  (Matthew 14:14 NIV)

- *"And his master's heart was moved with compassion, and he released him and forgave him [cancelling] the debt."*
  (Matthew 18:27, Amplified Bible)

- *"So Jesus had compassion and touched their eyes. And immediately their eyes received sight, and they followed Him."*
  (Matthew 20:34 NKJV)

How do these passages make you feel about the Jesus you serve? I know how they make me react. They make me want to serve people with divine compassion more than I already do.

A compassionate church

Christ first loved us and gave Himself up for us. He loves His Church and He longs for us to be a body of people who manifest His truth and compassion on earth. But as a Church we sometimes get things wrong, don't we? Sometimes we mean to show compassion, but we make mistakes. We are human, but we must keep trying to show divine and holy love to all who we come into contact with. We must value people for who they are, allowing them to know that they are part of God's unique story.

We have a very special steward at our church called Nigel. He is well-loved and appreciated for the amazing person that he is and the wonderful job that he does. The other stewards all baptised him and they take care of him like a family. When they go away on men's weekends together, they look after him and put him to bed. Nigel is a loving man with Down's syndrome. But he has a role to play in the life of the kingdom that is valued by God and by us. His very existence in our midst teaches us something precious about God's love and compassion.

I want to belong to the kind of church where anyone and everyone feels welcomed and valued. I want to welcome prostitutes and drug dealers, alcoholics and people with mental health problems. Maybe you have never felt part of God's community of believers for some reason? Maybe you feel you have let God down in some way that excludes you from His love and compassion, or from the acceptance of His people? But the truth is that the divine compassion of Christ is no respecter of persons. It doesn't shun you because you have had an abortion, been divorced a number of times, are unable to hold a job down or been dismissed for dishonesty. The love and compassion of Jesus reaches through and beyond those things. God loves you in this moment for who He has made you to be. He knows that we all foul up at times, but His compassion never fails.

Thinking it through:

◊ What are your compassion levels like? Do you have a heart of compassion for others?
◊ Do you struggle to feel that sense of deep love for others, or are you the kind of person to whom it comes naturally?

◊ Do you know Jesus' compassion for you?
◊ Can you think of a time when you acted out of compassion for another person? What happened?

Read the following passage and spend some time dwelling on what it tells you of divine compassion.

> "Then the LORD came down in the cloud and stood there with him and proclaimed his name, the LORD. And he passed in front of Moses, proclaiming, "The LORD, the LORD, the compassionate and gracious God, slow to anger, abounding in love and faithfulness, maintaining love to thousands, and forgiving wickedness, rebellion and sin."
>
> (Exodus 34:5-7 NIV)

What do you need to know from Him today?

Maybe you could spend some time asking Jesus for a fresh revelation of His compassion for you and for His lost world. You might like to note down anything He tells you.

> "At the end of life we will not be judged by how many diplomas we have received, how much money we have made, how many great things we have done. We will be judged by 'I was hungry and you gave me to eat, I was naked and you clothed me, I was homeless and you took me in.' Hungry not only for bread – but hungry for love. Naked not only for clothing – but naked for human dignity and respect. Homeless not only for want of a room of bricks – but homeless because of rejection."
>
> Mother Teresa

CHAPTER 14 *Righteousness*

"I will give thanks to the LORD because of his righteousness and will sing praise to the name of the LORD Most High."

(Psalm 7:17 NIV)

What is righteousness?

Righteousness is a matter of relationships – with God, with things and with others. The biblical definition of righteousness is tied to the inherent quality of our permanently righteous God. In all circumstances and all situations, God is perfectly right in His actions, expressions and desires. For us as Christians then, righteousness is about representing God's character by *being* right, *doing* right and *putting* right.

The Bible is very clear that we cannot do anything righteous in our own strength. Proverbs 16:25 says,

"There is a way that seems right to a man, but in the end it leads to death." NIV

But Scripture teaches us that if we seek God's kingly reign and His righteousness as our priority, all we need will be provided:

> *"Therefore do not worry, saying, 'What shall we eat?' or 'What shall we drink?' or 'What shall we wear?' ... For your heavenly Father knows that you need all these things. But seek first the kingdom of God and His righteousness, and all these things shall be added to you."*
>
> (Matthew 6:31-33 NKJV)

I believe that the greatest fight we will have every day of our lives is about our righteousness. In our conversations, our lifestyle, the way we react to people, or indeed how we respond to God: righteousness, or our lack of it, will be a defining factor.

Righteousness as friendship with God

In John 15:14 Jesus says,

> *"You are my friends if you do what I command."* NIV

Jesus, the "friend of sinners" who is truly righteous, offers us eternal friendship with Him *if* we do His will. Isn't that amazing? Very few of us would ever think of entering a friendship by working out such a contract. But Jesus did that with us. He told us everything that He expects of us and everything that we can expect of Him in our righteousness:

1. *"I'll never leave you or forsake you."*
   (Hebrews 13:5 NASB)
2. *"I am with you always even to the end of the age."*
   (Matthew 28:20 NASB)
3. *"I've got a better place for you."* (John 14:2 NASB)
4. *"I'll stick closer than a brother."*
   (Proverbs 18:24 NASB)

God's friendship is not based on an emotional bond, but on a righteous covenant relationship. It's written all through the Bible. God will never ask us to do anything or go anywhere that He hasn't equipped us for. Whatever He asks us to do we can achieve with His strength. If we lived with the knowledge of this friendship as the top priority in our lives, and the source of our righteousness, our churches would be inaccessible because of the crowds! The truth is we may desire it, but we don't strive for it enough.

Hungering for Righteousness

How thirsty and hungry are we for righteousness?
Matthew 5 recalls Jesus' sermon on the mount:

> *"Blessed are the poor in spirit, for theirs is the Kingdom of Heaven. Blessed are those who mourn, for they shall be comforted. Blessed are the meek, for they shall inherit the earth. Blessed are those who hunger and thirst for righteousness, for they shall be filled."*
> NKJV

The word "blessed" used here is the word *makarios* which means "something large or long in duration". Jesus is not saying we will be blessed for five minutes. This kind of blessing is not going to fade. Jesus is saying if we truly desire righteousness, hungering and thirsting after it, not only will we get it, but we will be *filled* with it. So what are we waiting for? Do we really want to be satisfied with this meal God is offering? I know I do!

You know that feeling when you're in the right place at the right time, doing the right thing in the right way? There's an incredible energy and joy over you. That sense of peace and righteousness is possible every day in Christ. Can you imagine all your thoughts, words and actions being right? No longer would you be the reason someone loses their way. You would not be offensive or unkind, nor would you be quick to take offence in return. I would love a lot more of that kind of righteousness in my life.

I received a letter this week that showed me how God had blessed a couple hungering for righteousness in their own lives:

"My husband was in a low-paid job, which meant we couldn't buy a house. He went to see his bosses and they didn't want to know. Last week we came to church and you encouraged us to shout out to God, reminding us that the 'prayer of a righteous man is powerful and effective' (James 5:16). So we shouted and asked God to break the walls down. On Thursday, my husband's boss called him in and said, 'We've been watching you closely. We're going to talk, at the end of the month, about giving you that pay rise.'"

See what happens when we hunger for righteousness? We will be FILLED! Amazing things will come when we do the right thing, at the right time, in the right way, for the right reasons.

Attacked for righteousness

Matthew 5:10-12 (NIV) makes it clear, however, that our righteousness will not protect us from attack. In fact we are to expect persecution and even learn to rejoice in it.

> *"Blessed are those who are persecuted because of righteousness, for theirs is the kingdom of heaven. Blessed are you when people insult you, persecute you and falsely say all kinds of evil against you because of me. Rejoice and be glad, because great is your reward*

in heaven, for in the same way they persecuted the prophets who were before you."

Notice it doesn't say: "Blessed are you IF people insult you." It says "WHEN". It is a forgone conclusion that our righteousness will cause some people to react very strongly indeed. It's not about us being persecuted for being rude and obnoxious. That's not righteousness. This is all about being attacked for getting things right, putting things right and acting rightly.

I was on a plane recently and got talking to a young Muslim engineer from Jordan. He asked me why I thought Christians, Muslims and Jews all fought over the same piece of land in Jerusalem. He told me, "We think we are right, but so does everyone else." Do you know what his solution to the problem was? He went on to say, "We could build a three-storey building on the holy site. The Jews can have one floor, the Christians can have another and we'll have the final one!" I said, "The only trouble is, son, everyone would argue over who got the top floor!" This is the way the world tries to do "righteousness". It is not about applying earthly logic. We have to go directly to God for the source of our righteousness before Him.

It is interesting that verses 11 and 12 of Matthew 5 speak about living above negative criticism – not living with pressure, hurt or bruising, but with blessing, rejoicing and choosing to be exceedingly glad. Why? Because the Christian should be the solution not the problem. We are, it goes on to say later in the passage, the salt and the light. We are a preservative and a flavour for our community. We are meant to be the light – that ray of hope and sunshine – in a place of darkness. We are a revelation of who Jesus is. We are righteousness in an unrighteous world, just as He was.

The freedom in righteousness

If we submitted to His righteousness we would be free of condemnation once and for all. We would not be living under judgement, neither judging others nor being judged. As it says in Galatians 3:24 (Amplified Bible),

> "So that the Law served [to us Jews] as our trainer [our guardian, our guide to Christ, to lead us] until Christ [came], that we might be justified (declared righteous, put in right standing with God) by and through faith."

Some of us have judged people so often we don't know how to stop. We judge everybody according to our own interpretation. But when we live in the righteousness of Christ we live in a state of FREEDOM!

FREEDOM from the penalty of sin!

FREEDOM from condemnation!

FREEDOM from limitation!

Whether we live in need or abundance, God stays the same. He never alters. If we've got cancer, He never alters. If we've got heart trouble, He never alters. If we lose our job, He never alters. He is always righteous.
Knowing that, brings us true and lasting freedom.

Righteousness – being like Him

I get rather fed up of people saying, when I speak and travel, "Pastor Dave, do you know you're one of the few people who has time to stop and talk to people?" This always surprises me because it's not a virtue in me – it's my responsibility!

Surely that is what Jesus did and what He wants us all to do?

To act in an unrighteous way towards people is not only a dishonour to them, but a sign of dissatisfaction with the values of Jesus. What we're saying when we treat others this way is, "Jesus, I don't trust in your values of forgiveness, reconciliation, kindness and gentleness – in fact, Jesus, you offend me!" Trust me, as I have been writing this I have found this so hard-hitting in my own life, that I have had to seriously think and pray!

If righteousness is the identification of the Christian, forgiveness and restoration are its daily function. We cannot be truly children of God unless we function in such a way. In Revelation 3:16 Jesus says,

"So, because you are lukewarm—neither hot nor cold—I am about to spit you out of my mouth." NIV

Please, God, may I not be lukewarm in my response to You or to others! I don't want to be so abhorrent to God that He has to spew me out! Don't get me wrong here. I know it's hard to remain righteous. Paul puts it very clearly in Romans 7:17-25:

"As it is, it is no longer I myself who do it, but it is sin living in me. I know that nothing good lives in me, that is, in my sinful nature. For I have the desire to do what is good, but I cannot carry it out. For what I do is not the good I want to do; no, the evil I do not want to do— this I keep on doing. Now if I do what I do not want to do, it is no longer I who do it, but it is sin living in me that does it.

So I find this law at work: When I want to do good, evil is right there with me. For in my inner being I

> *delight in God's law; but I see another law at work in the members of my body, waging war against the law of my mind and making me a prisoner of the law of sin at work within my members. What a wretched man I am! Who will rescue me from this body of death? Thanks be to God—through Jesus Christ our Lord!"* NIV

Paul is saying, "The things I want to do I can't do, and things I shouldn't do, I do!" We all have that same experience don't we? But look how Paul finishes this section. It is by believing that Jesus has the answer and the power.

Jesus was completely righteous, even in death. No one could find anything wrong with Him. There was nothing to accuse Him of. He remained silent. He didn't try to fight, explain or justify Himself. What was it about Him that caused a thief to turn to Him on the cross and think, "There's something about you I want?" It was His righteousness.

People can tell whether you're righteous, even if you don't open your mouth. Sometimes people will know you by what you *don't* say. When everyone else is gossiping or laughing at a lewd comment and you're not, they know you by what you don't do! Wouldn't that be a miracle for some of us? Imagine if you said, "I'm not going to open my mouth and be negative about anyone this week." Would your conversations be a lot shorter? Would your heart be more righteous before God?

Jesus' righteousness absorbs our unrighteousness

Whenever Jesus came into contact with sinners, His righteousness absorbed their unrighteousness so that they could become clean. Don't you just love that? Righteousness was a person they could see – not a concept on a scroll. His righteousness takes on our unrighteousness, but doesn't change His in the slightest. It's a bit like lighting a candle. You can light a candle from another candle without the first candle losing any of its brightness. That's what righteousness is like.

We too can be righteous amongst unrighteousness and not become sullied by it. We become and stay clean through His purity. We remain clean by living daily in His presence and surrounding ourselves with others who reflect Him. If we are struggling with the retention of genuine spiritual joy then it may be valuable to examine our own righteousness before blaming others. I often find that when people offend me, it tells me more about my level of righteousness than theirs!

In Matthew 7:1-1 Jesus says,

"Do not judge others, and you will not be judged. For you will be treated as you treat others. The standard you use in judging is the standard by which you will be judged." NLT

I want to qualify this. Jesus doesn't mean that we allow unrighteousness to run rampant. We address unrighteousness, but we don't judge the unrighteous. Christians rightly believe that homosexuality or adultery is wrong, but we're not going to attack the homosexual or the adulterer. Their sin is no worse than ours. We need to copy Christ and show them the compassion He would show. Jesus sat with the adulterer, not compromising Himself or His beliefs, but showing them His love and acceptance. Jesus sat with wine-drinkers but did not get drunk. Jesus sat with prostitutes but didn't sleep with them. He sat with cheats and did not cheat. We can do the same. But we need to come from a place of internal righteousness or we are likely to fall.

Staying in righteousness

Pastors and leaders fail all the time. They might get too "big for their boots", or not be able to handle all that God gives them through lack of self-knowledge or accountability. But when someone else is unrighteous, it is not our job to stop and pass judgement. We can be sad and prayerful, but we should not take the opportunity to dwell on their faults. After all, we have plenty of our own! I've been there myself – not always in the same circumstances as others, but I've had stuff that I couldn't handle and I've made a botch up of it. I'm sure you have too. But we have a loving and forgiving God, as well as a righteous God!

We don't understand righteousness until we understand sin. Righteousness is everything that sin isn't. In 1 John 3:4 John tells us that sin is lawlessness. This way of living is against the Law of God that Jesus died to fulfil.

Sadly, we all sin at times, but forgiveness, restoration, re-establishment and re-engaging with God is the normal Christian attitude expected by Christ. Countless stories that Jesus told give credence to such philosophy: the man in debt, who was forgiven much; the prodigal son, whose father's sacrificial love embraced his repentant son, but endured the smell and the stain of the pigsty; Zacchaeus giving his money to the poor ....

All through the Bible the Lord tells us to pursue, practise, touch, live out and speak out the righteousness we have in Him. God actually puts the onus back on us. We become people who are conduits for a miracle and open for a miracle. We become people who God can get through to.

A friend of mine, David Hicks, speaks of 4 different "items" or aspect of righteousness God gives us:

1. *A robe of righteousness* – *our clothes from Him*
(Job 29:14)
2. *A breastplate of righteousness* – *our protection in Him*
(Ephesians 6:14)
3. *A crown of righteousness* – *our position in Him*
(2 Timothy 4:8)
4. *A sceptre of righteousness* – *our authority from Him*
(Hebrews 1:8)

Isn't that an amazing set of truths? Look at what righteousness in Christ offers us?

When I was in Portland, USA, recently, the air was very clean and fresh. I noticed how good my breathing was. My sinuses felt so clear. But when I got off the plane in Birmingham, I started sneezing and became all clogged up again. We acclimatise to where we are. If we surround ourselves with righteous talk and righteous people it will affect our spiritual breathing in the same way. As Ephesians 6:14 declares, we need to cover our hearts with the breastplate of righteousness. Only this can truly protect what is in our hearts. When we pursue righteousness, it will clear and clean our souls. We will live in a healthier state, physically, spiritually, emotionally and mentally, ready for that miracle.

I am up for that! Are you?

Thinking it through:

> *"God has nothing to say to the self-righteous. Unless you humble yourselves before Him and you're prepared to come to the dust, and confess before Him your iniquities and sins, the gate of Heaven which is open for sinners saved by grace, must be shut against you forever."*
>
> D. L. Moody

General Schwarzkopf (who led the first military attack against Iraq) said, "The truth of the matter is that you always know the right thing to do, the hard part is doing it."

◊ What are the things you struggle to be righteous about?
◊ Is there something in your lifestyle that you struggle with? Perhaps it's an attitude, or a habit, a fear or a character trait.

It may help you to write that issue down and prayerfully commit it to God, asking Him for a fresh start in your journey of righteousness today. You may also like to use the words of this prayer:

"Lord, You are so righteous and holy. Only You are perfect in all Your ways. Because You are a Righteous God, I trust You that You are always planning my days for me. I know every good gift comes from You and that You will supply all of my needs according to Your eternal riches and wisdom. I praise You, Jesus, for taking my sin and giving me Your righteousness so that I can stand before God as blameless and holy. You, O Lord, are my righteousness. There is no good in me apart from You. Forgive me for where I have failed You and help me to seek after You and Your righteousness for my life. Help me to make wise decisions and to be a righteous and upright person, now and always. Amen."

CHAPTER 15
Integrity

The heart of integrity

We serve a God who is full of integrity and righteousness. In all His ways, His desires and His thinking, He shows His unchanging and consistent character – to be the same "yesterday, today and forever" (Hebrews 13:8). But how can we be people of true integrity too?

What kind of person has real integrity? Think of someone in your own life who you would say has this authority about them. Perhaps it is someone who keeps their word, who is faithful, who makes careful decisions, who chooses their friends and words wisely. A person of biblical integrity is a Christian who does the right thing *even when no one is watching*. A person of integrity also has self-awareness and self-knowledge.

Matthew 7:2-4 (NIV) says,

> *"For in the same way as you judge others, you will be judged, and with the measure you use, it will be measured to you. Why do you look at the speck of sawdust in your brother's eye and pay no attention to the plank in your own eye? How can you say to your brother, 'Let me take the speck out of your eye,' when all the time there is a plank in your own eye?"*

We need to note here that Jesus does not say to *ignore* the speck in your brother's eye, He says, *first* take the plank out of your own, *then* you will be able to see clearly enough to judge what else needs removing. Having integrity isn't just about being able to discern what is going on with other people. It is about understanding what we are like too.

Matthew 7:7-8 says,

> *"Ask and it will be given to you; seek and you will find; knock and the door will be opened to you. For everyone who asks receives; he who seeks finds; and to him who knocks, the door will be opened."*   NIV

How many times have we read that scripture and nonchalantly thought it was meant for us? After all, it does say "everyone". But it bears closer scrutiny. I don't think we can use and quote that scripture unless we live lives of righteousness and integrity. God says, "What's your life like? Are you judgemental? Are you righteous? What's the measure of your integrity – in your conversation, in your actions, in your deeds, in your spirituality, in your finances, in your sexuality … are you righteous? Because if you are, ask and you will receive. Seek and you will find. But if not, it's not going to happen. Don't ask."

How often have you said to your children when they speak to you, "Ask me in the right way please!" I can remember my Mum saying that frequently to me: "Ask properly!" Then I'd say, "Excuse me, Mum, can I have …?" And if you had a Mum like mine she'd say, "No!"! (My Mum was a law unto herself, bless her heart!)

Living a life of integrity

I believe that God says to us, "If you are prepared to act righteously and live with integrity, you can ask and you will receive." If you're sick today, you can ask of Him. If you need guidance today, you can ask of Him. If you ask in the right way, it *will* be given or added to your life. Jesus is addressing a source of deception or self-denial here. Sometimes we react to others in a given situation and seek to find fault with them in order to justify our own actions. Haven't we all done that? I've lost count of the times I've heard people say, "Well, Pastor Dave, if you knew what I had to put up with ... if you'd heard what they said about me ... if you knew what they'd done, you would react like I have." Sometimes, even if people acknowledge their faults, they seek to justify them saying, "Yeah, I know I've got problems ... I know I'm not perfect ... I'm only human."

I've got news for you "only-humans" out there. With that attitude you won't inherit the Kingdom of God! If you try and knock the door and say, "I'm only human!" God could well say to you, "You can't get in here then!" If we try to bring our humanity into our spirituality like this, we are simply bringing the flesh in to justify our own actions. Jesus has come to take away the need to do that, to lift us from the fallen state of our humanity and to bring us into righteous integrity and holiness with Him.

I've always said this: when somebody does something in your life that upsets you, what you should actually do (when you've got over the shock) is go over and thank them! They've just shown you a little more of who you are. A young minister was incredibly offensive to me recently, terribly rude. But rather than argue with him, I felt it right to say, "You've just been very offensive to me. I'm going to walk away from you."

If I'm honest, years ago I would have got him by the throat and punched his lights out! My temper would have snapped – just like that! Plus, I'd have held it against him forever and a day. But in this situation I felt challenged by God to be a man of integrity. So, I took him out for a meal to talk about what had been said and put it right. I'm not saying this to exalt myself. What I'm saying is, how can I preach and write about this today if I don't live it? I'm just a basic Christian, but I've learnt over the years that I'd better practise what I preach and preach what I practise!

How often though, do we get things like that wrong? Someone hurts us and it's always *them* with the problem. It's always someone else who's made us miserable, withdrawn, critical – it's always their fault. No, *we* have a choice in how we react. This is really important to remember: nobody can offend you, you choose to *take* offence. You have a decision to make about how you will handle difficult people and hard situations. You can choose to be a person of integrity, or not.

Obviously it can be very painful when people are offensive to us. It's not nice when people say things behind our back, but the way we react to situations like that shows God who we are. And can we honestly say that we have never done the same? Some of us are terrible gossips: "sharing" items with others "for prayer". What a load of rubbish that can be at times! We aren't giving the information to help that person at all. The motivation is to feel better about ourselves! Some of us refuse to think of ourselves as gossips. The way we speak and the topics we speak about are so second nature to us, we have no clue we are gossiping at all. As far as we are concerned we are simply "airing our opinion". But would we honestly say exactly the same thing if that person were in the room? I doubt it. Gossip, is like a cancer of the soul that destroys more people than cancer of the body. I think it has the potential to rot your soul, and the soul of the person you're talking about.

Somebody once phoned me by mistake, having dialled my number without realising it. I answered and heard the person talking about a conversation they'd had with me! To this day they don't realise that I heard it. I just sat there listening to it all and then I hung up the phone. Now I know the painful truth of what they think of me, but I've had to let it go. God has a wonderful way of exposing things, doesn't He?

Sometimes it is hard to have integrity when other people won't change or allow themselves to be reconciled with us when we've had a disagreement. Matthew 18:15-16 gives us clear instructions about such disputes:

> *"If your brother sins against you, go and show him his fault, just between the two of you. If he listens to you, you have won your brother over. But if he will not listen, take one or two others along, so that every matter may be established by the testimony of two or three witnesses."* NIV

I've pastored a church for 38 years and I know only a handful of Christians who have ever done what this scripture tells us. We whinge and whine and go to the Pastor. We tell our friends and we ignore our new enemy. Perhaps we react out of fear, but often it is stinking pride that gets in the way. The devil loves to bring disunity into the Body of Christ. It's one of his favourite hobbies.

Meanwhile, we have the opportunity to "gain a brother" from a horrible situation. Isn't that a wonderful thing? You can have a unity that you've never had before. If you haven't gone to lecture him, but you've arrived in a manner that will actually enable him to respond, look what you have won. You can say something like, "Now, it may be me and my sensitivity – and I'm sure you didn't mean it – but something transpired between us that has left me hurt. I just wanted to come and see you about it because, unless I'm wrong, I don't think you meant to do it." We should never wade in with, "Call yourself a Christian? You better get your act sorted out, mate!" That person will then begin to try to defend himself: "Don't you dare speak to me like that!" Then the whole thing will escalate. Churches have been decimated for less than this. When we are people of integrity we don't take our hurt with us. We leave it behind and lean hard on God's grace. Grace says, "I'm sure you didn't mean it."

If someone will not hear your plea, there's another procedure – you take with you one or two more to establish what has happened. Not your friends who will help beat him up – Jesus is not suggesting we take the heavy mob round! It's best to choose someone who is discerning and impartial, who might actually see things as they are and help you to act with integrity.

The source of our integrity

Don't forget, when God made the world He said it was "good". His heart is not to walk around slapping us! He wants to bless us. Some of us find it hard to believe that God actually likes us as well as loves us! He's our friend. We're His children. He's our Lord. He's our King. He's our High Priest. He's our Healer. He's our Provider. He's our Refuge. He's our Guide. He's our righteousness and our source of integrity.

The Bible tells us that when we see Him, we are going to be like Him – as full of holiness and integrity as He is:

1 John 3:1-3 says:

> *"How great is the love the Father has lavished on us, that we should be called children of God! And that is what we are! The reason the world does not know us is that it did not know him. Dear friends, now we are children of God, and what we will be has not yet been*

made known. But we know that when he appears, we shall be like him, for we shall see him as he is. Everyone who has this hope in him purifies himself, just as he is pure." NIV

This hope actually purifies us and makes us more likely to be people of goodness, righteousness, mercy, justice and integrity. He stands in the valley of death *with* us. He already waits in Paradise for us. If that's not a God who cares, then what is? Isn't it worth living a righteous life for a God like that? Isn't it worth dying to our own silly, selfish, stupid ways?

Psalm 78:72 (KJV) shows us God's passionate love for us in these precious words:

"So He fed them according to the integrity of His heart; and guided them by the skilfulness of His hands."

Even Jesus' enemies recognised that He was a man of righteousness and integrity, as this passage from Matthew 22:16 shows:

"They sent their disciples to him along with the Herodians. 'Teacher,' they said, 'we know you are a man of integrity and that you teach the way of God in accordance with the truth. You aren't swayed by men, because you pay no attention to who they are.'" NIV

Last week I had two different men come to see me. One said that he had been backslidden as a Christian for 6 years and had heard the Word and realized how far he had fallen. The other man said, "I've been a Christian for many years, Pastor Dave. But I have no integrity or righteousness. I feel so confused."

I said, "What is the source of your confusion?"

"I think God is telling me I am not actually a Christian!" the man said, sadly.

"Go with what God says," I told him. "He is more to be trusted than man. Why not get born again tonight?" And the man did.

Those two men realized that they were not living a righteous or a godly lifestyle. They had no integrity and when they heard the Word of God, they became convicted of its truth. Wasn't God merciful to them? He gave them another opportunity to put things right in their lives. God is the source of our right standing before Him. He is the only foundation for our integrity. Without Him, we are nothing but filthy rags.

Just because we talk the talk or have a gift, or even speak in tongues, doesn't mean we have integrity on the inside. I watched a very sad video this morning about a boy protégé who at the age of 4 became a leading Pentecostal evangelist. But the film showed how, as he grew up, he faked the whole lot, falsifying speaking in tongues, lying so that he could take all the offerings.

God knows the genuine article, even if we don't spot it. He will judge people according to their deeds. We need to remember, some of us, that we are dead a lot longer than we are alive! Unless we have loving integrity, we cannot please God.

We have a lovely man in our church. He hasn't been a Christian many years and he shared his testimony with us this week. He is a very open, honest man and told us he had a severe temper. One day this week he went to work, as he had done every day for 36 years, and the management told the workers that 100 of them were being made redundant. Knowing his normal nature, he spoke to one of his managers and said, "When I go and see the boss, will you come with me so that you can hold me back when I blow my stack?"

I told you he was an honest man! The boss told him that he had lost his job. He said nothing. Then he said, "May I just share my thoughts? I think this business has failed because you have been unrighteous and shown a lack of integrity in the following areas ..." Then very calmly, he listed the issues, as he saw them, in a controlled manner. Then he spoke again saying, "You know me and you know that I have a bad temper. I can see you are wondering why I haven't blown up. It's because my Pastor was speaking on righteousness and integrity last week. I've learnt that if I am righteous before God and if I speak and act and think in a way that demonstrates integrity, He will take care of me."

Then he turned and left the office.

Nothing I preached on was complicated at all. But the Word of God has power to change lives, doesn't it? Simple teaching has a profound effect. Some of us need to go back to basics.

Integrity is for NOW!

In Matthew 3:13-15 we read this:

> *"Then Jesus came from Galilee to the Jordan to be baptised by John. But John tried to deter him, saying, 'I need to be baptised by you, and do you come to me?' Jesus replied, 'Let it be so now; it is proper for us to do this to fulfil all righteousness.' Then John consented."*
>
> NIV

Jesus comes to river to be baptized, but John tries to stop Him. Why? I think he did not really understand who he was in God. Some people are waiting for God to use them and wonder why He hasn't, because they think they're brilliant! But most of us think the opposite. Our problem isn't arrogance, but false identity. We genuinely don't think we are qualified to do anything for God.

John simply did not see himself as God saw him. But look at how Jesus treats him. He says, "Let it be so *now*." Jesus understood that this was a "now" moment. This was His time.

Isn't it sad that we don't always know what God thinks of us and so miss our potential to serve Him? That false perspective is cumulative. We start to speak words over ourselves such as:

I can't!
I shouldn't!
I won't!
I'll never!

But Jesus speaks into that falsehood and says, "Let it be so *now*." Why did Jesus need to be baptized at that moment? He had reached the age of 30, the Jewish age of inheritance. He knew that His ministry was about to begin and He wanted to symbolize that in washing and starting again. There has to be a "now" moment in all of our lives. There has to be a "now" time when we are born again, when we become filled with the Spirit, when we start to live in obedience and integrity.

If you are a parent, you will know how necessary the word NOW is for your children. If you say to your children, "Come and eat" and you don't add the word NOW, your children may never come! How often have you said, "Go to bed NOW!" because you know that if you don't, NOW will never come? Children are soon wise to this and learn how many times you will say NOW before you REALLY mean it! If they work out that you don't mean NOW until the fifth time, they will keep you waiting.

But when God says NOW, we need to obey. He only says it once.

2 Corinthians 6:2 says,

> *"I tell you, **now** is the time of God's favour, now is the day of salvation."*
>
> NIV

When God brings a "now" into a life, He means NOW!

If Jesus hadn't been baptized, Heaven wouldn't have opened. We need an open heaven of blessing over our churches, businesses and families, don't we? But then we need to be people who hear the Word and do it, people who obey God's instruction and follow His words.

It is often not in the big things that God seeks our integrity and obedience. Recently, I received a letter from a man saying that, if I went out to visit a certain charismatic expression of renewal in America, I would come back and raise the dead. He meant well, but he wasn't speaking with God's authority and righteousness. When I went to my Bible to pray about that word, the Lord told me not to go and said that He would bless me at home.

How many times, with good intentions, do we stop the work of God in our lives because we have not listened to Him and not obeyed Him? God's right path for us may make us uncomfortable because it is contrary to our own, but it is always *right*.

Integrity needs honesty

In order to be people of true integrity we really need to be honest with ourselves. The trouble is, we can be blind and deaf and dumb to our own faults, can't we? We don't dare ask anyone to tell us our faults, just in case they actually do!

No one likes hearing the honest truth about themselves. Look at the X Factor on TV, for example. Most of the people on that show would make beautiful burglar alarms! Their voices would scare anyone off, but until they appeared on the show, no one had ever had the gall to tell them. So they go on national TV and are humiliated to discover that they have been lied to.

Counselling Christians can be a bit like the X Factor too. There are times when people ask me to be straight and honest with them. And I am! It's not my education or upbringing or a certain skill in me. I do it because it is what God asks of me. I seek to be a man of integrity. It's a bit like at the marriage of Cana in John 2. Mary says to the servants in verse 5,

"Do whatever he tells you."

NIV

That's what integrity is. It is no more complex than that.

If we are righteous and live in a way that pleases God, we seem to accidentally become successful. That happened to me in my business. The guys I worked with said, "You are so lucky, Dave. It's very unfair. Why does God do that for you?"

It happens now when I play bowls too. If I'm having a good day, they say, "God's helping you out today, Dave!" Of course, if I miss a lot of shots they also comment, "Where's God today then, mate?"

Either way, I don't get any credit at all! If we live a life of integrity we don't get either credit or blame. God takes us through our good days and bad days and He stays the same.

People come to me sometimes and lose their temper, then apologise saying, "I don't know what made me say that." I do – secretly they believed it so they said it! We are at our most honest when we lose our temper. We get embarrassed and try to cover it up. But actually it came from the heart.

Paul speaks in 1 Timothy 6:3-5 warning him to flee things that would compromise his righteousness and integrity:

> *"If anyone teaches false doctrines and does not agree to the sound instruction of our Lord Jesus Christ and to godly teaching, he is conceited and understands nothing. He has an unhealthy interest in controversies and quarrels about words that result in envy, strife, malicious talk, evil suspicions and constant friction between men of corrupt mind, who have been robbed of the truth and who think that godliness is a means to financial gain."*
>
> NIV

All these work against righteousness. But it is not enough to simply flee from them. We must also:

> *"... pursue righteousness, godliness, faith, love, endurance and gentleness. Fight the good fight of the faith. Take hold of the eternal life to which you were called."*
>
> (1 Timothy 6:11-12 NIV)

Paul is not talking about simply fleeing from sinfulness and unrighteousness, but actively pursuing a life of integrity and taking hold of the life to which we are called. Lives that are submitted to God in this way are full of the fruits of the Spirit, demonstrating God's power and a love for others, being shaped and characterised by integrity.

It's not about filling in a little response card at church or going on an Alpha course. We need to be clothed with a robe of righteousness, clothes we wear every day (see Isaiah 61:10).

Spencer Johnson said: "Integrity is telling yourself the truth, and honesty is telling the truth to others." Integrity is not about human effort it is about human obedience. I want people to look at my life and everything I am and see me as a man after God's heart, a man of truth and integrity. How about you?

Thinking it through:

◊ In what areas of your life do you think you lack integrity?
◊ Do you find it easy to gossip or speak loosely?
◊ Do you speak about yourself in an unhealthy way?
◊ What do you think God is asking you to pursue in your daily life?
◊ How can you make that a reality?

"Father, Your Word I have hidden in my heart that I might not sin against You; for it teaches me to do justly, to love mercy, and to walk humbly before You. Even when it brings about hurtful circumstances, help me to do the right thing in keeping with the Christ-filled nature I received upon the day of my salvation. May I not be found lacking in integrity but rather be characterized by my integrity as it honours my Father in heaven. In Jesus' name I pray, Amen."

Steven C. Weber

CHAPTER

16 *Majestic Glory*

What is glory?

What do you picture when you hear the word "glory"? For me it conjures up a revelation of God's unlimited abundance, His powerful presence with no restriction or boundary.

In Psalm 8:1 (Amplified Version) it says,

"Lord, our Lord, how excellent (majestic and glorious) is Your name in all the earth! You have set Your glory on (or above) the heavens."

C.S. Lewis said this:

"A man can no more diminish God's glory by refusing to worship Him than a lunatic can put out the sun by scribbling the word 'darkness' on the walls of his cell."

We cannot diminish the glory of the Lord, but we also cannot fathom it either. It is one of those things that cannot be quantified or explained easily. If we were able to grasp even a small amount of understanding regarding the majesty of God, we would live so very differently! When we pray, we often pray according to our circumstances and what we can see, and process things logically. It is much harder for us to pray with the glory of God in mind! We are conditioned by the limits of our humanity rather than by the majestic expanse of eternity. But if we learnt to live above "see level" we would uncover some amazing truths.

The *glory* of the Lord speaks of the depths of His wealth or treasure. We often forget this too. Be honest with me a minute. How often have you prayed this kind of prayer: "If You do this for me, Lord, I'll promise I'll do that"? Not just me, then! We try and barter with God sometimes. But God's glory means He can have anything He wants. We can't buy Him and we certainly won't get through to Him by trying to bribe Him. He's complete as He is and needs nothing we can offer.

Glory also refers to God's brightness and majesty. This is the Greek word *doza*, which means literally, "the bliss of heaven". What a beautiful thing! If we love God we are going to see a manifestation of His awesomeness in eternity.

Another variant of this word is *doxa* or in Hebrew *kavowd*. Both literally mean "weightiness", but carry the sense of "honour intended for God, not for man." God permits us and welcomes us into His glory, but it's not for us to take. It's majesty and eminence which radiate from God's own being.

"They shall speak of the glory of Your kingdom,
And talk of Your power,
To make known to the sons of men His mighty acts,
And the glorious majesty of His kingdom."
(Psalm 145:11-12 NKJV)

"Then your light shall break forth like the morning,
Your healing shall spring forth speedily,
And your righteousness shall go before you;
The glory of the LORD shall be your rear guard."
(Isaiah 58:8 NKJV)

Did you know that God's abundance, God's splendour, God's awesomeness and God's majestic glory are protecting you? Isn't that an incredible promise?

Martin Luther King understood this when he said:

> *"I have a dream that one day every valley shall be exalted, every hill and mountain shall be made low, the rough places will be made plain, and the crooked places will be made straight, and the glory of the Lord shall be revealed, and all flesh shall see it together."*
>
> (Based on Isaiah 40:4)

He didn't say, "I have a dream that every black person will have a vote...", although that's what he was working towards. He died having a dream of the glory of the Lord coming upon the earth.

The goodness of God's glory

In Exodus 33:15-20 we read an amazing passage that tells us something else about what God revealed in His glory:

> *"Then Moses said to him, 'If your Presence does not go with us, do not send us up from here. How will anyone know that you are pleased with me and with your people unless you go with us? What else will distinguish me and your people from all the other people on the face of the earth?' And the LORD said to Moses, 'I will do the very thing you have asked, because I am pleased with you and I know you by name.' Then Moses said, 'Now show me your glory.' And the LORD said, 'I will cause all my goodness to pass in front of you, and I will proclaim my name, the LORD, in your presence. I will have mercy on whom I will have mercy, and I will have*

compassion on whom I will have compassion. But,' he said, 'you cannot see my face, for no-one may see me and live." NIV

Beyond all the things he could have asked for, Moses only wanted to see God in His glory. God replies by saying, "I will cause all my GOODNESS to pass in front of you." Can you imagine what that must have looked and felt like? From this we can see that the power of God's glory is tied up in the purposes and presence of His very character. Before we get to the point of experiencing God's glory we've got to realise afresh that He is a good God. God chooses to display His goodness in His glory.

We can do this too.

Philippians 1:11 (Amplified Bible) says,

"May you abound in and be filled with the fruits of righteousness (of right standing with God and right doing) which come through Jesus Christ (the Anointed One), to the honour and praise of God (that His glory may be both manifested and recognized)."

I remember an amazing example of this in our church a while back. A man came to the church who'd had a breakdown. He'd gone to the Hebridean Islands with his family, as far away from things as he could get, and pored over his tattered life. Whilst sitting in a little cottage, he found and read a Bible. Finding answers for his questions and peace for his soul, he gave his life to the Lord and then hitchhiked to Solihull where his mother lived. He tried to find a job to support his family back in the Hebrides. He found work cutting the grass at a sewage farm, which was owned by a local Water Authority.

One day he was sitting in church and found himself talking to a man who asked him what he did. He told him he worked for the Severn Trent Water Authority. "That's funny," was the reply, "so do I. What's your name?"

"Alistair. I cut the grass at the sewage plant. What's your name?"

"I'm John ———." he answered.

Alistair was shocked because he knew that *this* John was the man in charge of the water company.

Alistair explained how he had ended up working there: all about his breakdown and the cottage up in the Hebrides where his family lived, and that he was working to try and raise the money to bring them down, so that they could live together. As he was listening to Alistair's story, John said, "Come to my house for tea."

He took him home, gave him a lovely meal and heard that he'd just become a Christian. He then gave him the keys to his brand new, top-of-the-range Saab, told him to take two weeks off work, gave him money and told him to go and get his family and bring them back to stay at his house. Alistair said, "How can I do that? You're my boss!"

John said, "You don't understand: you're now my brother."

That's the compassion and goodness that the glory of God shows us. Jesus said to His followers: "I've prepared a house for you" (John 14:2). Why would He do that? He's the boss! He's the King of kings and the Lord of lords. But He is also our brother.

The desire of Moses was not riches. He'd already walked away from that. He didn't want fame, even though he was the leader of over 1 million people. He chose to see the glory of God, and was shown the favour and goodness of God within that. I want to see that for myself, don't you?

The *shekinah* of God's glory

When we read passages like this one from Deuteronomy, we can see the truth that God's very presence dwells in His glory:

> *"So it was, when you heard the voice from the midst of the darkness, while the mountain was burning with fire, that you came near to me, all the heads of your tribes and your elders. And you said: 'Surely the LORD our God has shown us His glory and His greatness, and we have heard His voice from the midst of the fire. We have seen this day that God speaks with man; yet he still lives. Now therefore, why should we die? For this great fire will consume us; if we hear the voice of the LORD our God anymore, then we shall die. For who is there of all flesh who has heard the voice of the living God speaking from the midst of the fire, as we have, and lived? 'You go near and hear all that the LORD our God may say, and tell us all that the LORD our God says to you, and we will hear and do it.' Then the LORD heard the voice of your words when you spoke to me, and the LORD said to me: 'I have heard the voice of the words of this people which they have spoken to you. They are right in all that they have spoken. Oh, that they had such a heart in them that they would fear Me and always keep all My commandments, that it might be well with them and with their children forever! Go and say to them, "Return to your tents." 'But as for you, stand here by Me, and I will speak to you all the commandments, the statutes, and the judgments which you shall teach them, that they may observe them in the land which I am giving them to possess.'*
>
> *"Therefore you shall be careful to do as the LORD your*

God has commanded you; you shall not turn aside to the right hand or to the left. You shall walk in all the ways which the LORD your God has commanded you, that you may live and that it may be well with you, and that you may prolong your days in the land which you shall possess."
(Deuteronomy 5:23-33 NKJV)

What an experience! There was no intercessor to broker sinful man's entrance into the kingdom. But it was in the Old Testament that the *shekinah* glory of God, which means "the dwelling presence", decided to dwell amongst men. How wonderful it would be if we had more of that – a visible manifestation of His presence!

"So they took their journey from Succoth and camped in Etham at the edge of the wilderness. And the LORD went before them by day in a pillar of cloud to lead the way, and by night in a pillar of fire to give them light, so as to go by day and night. He did not take away the pillar of cloud by day or the pillar of fire by night from before the people."
(Exodus 13:20-22 NKJV)

This was the visible presence of His glory: cloud and fire. In 1 Kings 8:12 when Solomon spoke,

"The LORD said He would dwell in the dark cloud."
NKJV

We see this mirrored in the New Testament at the time of Jesus' death on the cross.

On the day of Pentecost we see the appearance of God's glory in the flames of fire over the disciples' heads. The glory of the Lord was in both places. If ever Jesus needed to know that God was majestic and glorious it was just before He died. It's the same with us. If ever we need to know that He's paid the price, it's at death. If ever we want to know the glorious splendour of the King and that He's gone to prepare a place for us, it's when we face our own mortality.

Similarly, if ever the disciples needed to know the glory of God, it was in that upper room soon after they had despaired because of the death of Jesus. Suddenly, God's glory appeared and they were filled with boldness. Being surrounded by God's glory dramatically changes how we see things.

The power of God's glory

Moses was a young man who was full of ambition. He'd tried to do things his own way, killing a man in anger and ending up a fugitive. God called him through the burning bush (Exodus 3), telling him to take his shoes off as it was holy ground. He didn't even know who God was!

That fire revealed the abundance of God's glory to Moses. The voice of the Divine spoke. And yet the bush was not consumed. The way in which God reveals His glory to us is powerful and demands a response, and yet it does not destroy us:

It came to pass....

> "....when they lifted up their voice with the trumpets and cymbals and instruments of music, and praised the LORD, saying: 'For He is good, for His mercy endures forever,' that the house, the house of the LORD, was filled with a cloud, so that the priests could not continue

ministering because of the cloud; for the glory of the LORD filled the house of God."
(2 Chronicles 5:13-14 NKJV)

"When Solomon had finished praying, fire came down from heaven and consumed the burnt offering and the sacrifices; and the glory of the LORD filled the temple. And the priests could not enter the house of the LORD, because the glory of the LORD had filled the LORD's house. When all the children of Israel saw how the fire came down, and the glory of the LORD on the temple, they bowed their faces to the ground on the pavement, and worshiped and praised the LORD, saying: 'For He is good, For His mercy endures forever.'"
(2 Chronicles 7:1-3 NKJV)

I don't want to knock any so-called "revivals" that may be taking place, but a lot of them seem to make a lot of noise and put on a big show. I don't see much majestic glory in what's going on in some churches in the world. I just see a spectacle that, if I'm honest, makes me feel sick.

What happens when real *revival* comes is that the glory of God comes in! People aren't the centre of attention, dressed up smart because they are being filmed on Christian TV. They are simply on their faces before God! That kind of power is what is going to heal the sick and keep them healed; that is what's going to restore marriages and bind up the broken-hearted. It's not us putting on some kind of performance, it's the majesty of God running rampant in His house!

When we sing and worship as one and begin to pray to the Lord, then the power of His presence comes. I'm believing that one day we won't just fall down at the front of our churches when we pray, but we'll fall down on the pavement outside by the bus stop! Can you understand me getting so passionate about this? I'm not prepared to take empty old religion. That's not God's powerful glory. I'm 65 – I don't want to be the generation that has to die to see the glory of God. I want to see the glory of God *now* in the land of the living like Isaiah did!

> *"In the year that King Uzziah died, I saw the Lord sitting on a throne, high and lifted up, and the train of His robe filled the temple."*
>
> (Isaiah 6:1 NKJV)

Worshipping God for His glory

Not only is God full of glory, but we can give glory back to Him. We can treat Him with the majesty and honour He deserves and acknowledge His abundant grace with limitless praise.

> *"And behold, an angel of the Lord stood before them, and the glory of the Lord shone around them, and they were greatly afraid. Then the angel said to them, 'Do not be afraid, for behold, I bring you good tidings of great joy which will be to all people. For there is born to you this day in the city of David a Savior, who is Christ the Lord. And this will be the sign to you: You will find a Babe wrapped in swaddling cloths, lying in a manger.' And suddenly there was with the angel a multitude of the heavenly host praising God and saying: 'Glory to God in the highest, And on earth peace, goodwill toward men!'"*
>
> (Luke 2:9-14 NKJV)

These humble shepherds were filled with the kind of awesome fear that is completely missing in the Church right now. We are sometimes in danger of treating God like some kind of "high-fiving" sports coach! These men were exposed to a glimpse of heaven. The glory of the Lord shone around them. Paul was blinded by that glory. Moses had this glory pass before him and was told that if he looked on it he would die. God told him to hide himself in the cleft of the rock. He provided a safe way for His goodness and His glory to pass by and bless Moses.

God does the same thing for us today.

Augustus Toplady, in 1776, was overtaken by a thunderstorm in Burrington Coombe, Mendip. He penned a hymn, "Rock of Ages, cleft for me, let me hide myself in thee …" This hymn was sung at the funeral of William Gladstone in Westminster Abbey. Prince Albert, as he was waiting to die, asked for a choir to come and sing this to him. When the ship *The London* went down in the Bay of Biscay on January 11th 1866, the last thing that they heard, as it went down, was the voices of the passengers singing *Rock of Ages*.

> "Rock of Ages, cleft for me,
> let me hide myself in Thee;
> let the water and the blood,
> from thy wounded side which flowed,
> be of sin the double cure;
> save from wrath and make me pure.
> Not the labours of my hands
> can fulfil Thy law's commands;
> could my zeal no respite know,
> could my tears forever flow,
> all for sin could not atone;
> Thou must save, and Thou alone.

*Nothing in my hand I bring,
simply to the cross I cling;
naked, come to Thee for dress;
helpless, look to Thee for grace;
foul, I to the fountain fly;
wash me, Saviour, or I die.
While I draw this fleeting breath,
when mine eyes shall close in death,
when I soar to worlds unknown,
see Thee on Thy judgment throne,
Rock of Ages, cleft for me,
let me hide myself in Thee."*

God's desire is that we hide ourselves in this majestic glory; that we live in the power and the awesomeness of His character. We all need more of a manifestation of this in our own lives, don't we? God's glory will not destroy us but it will demand a response. It's that glory that will bring you wholeness and healing; it's that glory that will deliver you from the valley of the shadow of death; it's that glory that will bring you into the place called Paradise; it's that glory that will enter us into the very heart of heaven.

Thinking it through:

◊ Do you know the glory of the Lord in your life, in your family, in your business, in your church, and in your body?

◊ Are you going through a dark time, with a thunderous cloud and cracking storm over you? Do you have blessed assurance that Jesus is yours?

He can deliver you from drug addiction, can save you from an immoral life and cleanse you from all those mistakes you've made. He can release you from your intellectualism, that has only caused you to ask questions and never answered any that really meant anything.

Why not dwell on the words of this prayer:

"Father God, I want to thank You that when Moses asked to see Your glory, You were gracious to him. You showed him Your goodness and revealed Yourself to him. You showed him grace and compassion and then You placed him in a rock, which was very close to You.

That rock is now Jesus Christ, very close to You, and as we stand in that rock and Your glory passes by, we're safe, we're secure, both now and when we die. I turn now and cling to the majestic glory of the Rock of Ages. Amen."

We hope you enjoyed reading this
New Wine book.
For details of other New Wine books
and a wide range of titles from other
Word and Spirit publishers visit our website:
www.newwineministries.co.uk
or e mail us on newwine@xalt.co.uk